FAMILY ALBUM

for Americans

A nostalgic return to the venturesome life of America's yesterdays

by Michael and Vera Kraus

A Ridge Press Book | Grosset & Dunlap
NEW YORK

FAMILY ALBUM

for Americans *A nostalgic return to the venturesome life of America's yesterdays*

by Michael and Vera Kraus *A Ridge Press Book* | Grosset & Dunlap
NEW YORK

Prepared and produced by Ridge Press, Inc.
Published by Grosset & Dunlap, Inc.
© 1961 by Ridge Press, Inc.
Library of Congress Catalogue Number 61-13009
Printed in the United States of America

Editor-in-Chief: JERRY MASON
Editor: ADOLPH SUEHSDORF
Art Director: ALBERT A. SQUILLACE
Project Editor: EDWINA HAZARD GLEN
Associate Editor: RUTH BIRNKRANT
Associate Editor: EVELYN HANNON
Art Researcher: PETER LACEY
Art Associate: LEON BOLOGNESE
Production: ALLIED GRAPHIC ARTS

Contents

FOR MOTHER

Among the sources used in this volume are: Andy Adams: The Log of a Cowboy (1903); Lewis Atherton: Main Street on the Middle Border (1954); D. W. Brogan: The American Character (1959); R. C. Buley: The Old Northwest: Pioneer Period—1815-1840 (1950), 2 vols.; Thomas D. Clark: Pills, Petticoats and Plows (1944); David Cohn: The Good Old Days (1940); Marshall Davidson: Life in America (1951), 2 vols.; Everett Dick: The Sod-House Frontier—1854-1890 (1937); Seymour Dunbar: A History of Travel in America (1937); Philip Graham: Showboats (1951); David Lavender: Land of Giants: The Drive to the Pacific Northwest (1958); W. Storrs Lee: The Yankees of Connecticut (1957); Frank Moss: The American Metropolis: New York City Life (1897), 3 vols.; Earl Pomeroy: In Search of the Golden West (1957); Constance Rourke: American Humor (1953); Fred A. Shannon: The Farmer's Last Frontier 1860-1897 (1945); Mark Sullivan: Our Times: The Turn of the Century (1928); Warren S. Tryon: A Mirror for Americans (1952), 3 vols.; Bernard A. Weisberger: They Gathered at the River (1958); also various volumes in The History of American Life (D. R. Fox and A. M. Schlesinger, eds., 1927-1943).

The editors wish to extend grateful appreciation to the following people for their generous assistance: Donald Brenwasser, who photographed most of the color pictures; Louis Stark, and his staff in the Rare Book Room of the New York Public Library; Arthur B. Carlson, Paul Bride, and Carolyn Scoon, of the New York Historical Society; Albert K. Baragwanath and Henriette Beal, of the Museum of the City of New York; Albert Reese, of the Kennedy Galleries, Inc.; Mrs. Alden Shuman, of the Metropolitan Museum of New York; Huntington Cairns and Betty S. Gajdusek, of the National Gallery of Art, Washington, D.C.
Thanks should also be given to the staffs of all the other institutions listed among the picture credits.

The Background

A thirteen-gun salute began the city's welcome. All the way from Mount Vernon, accompanied by mounted troops, he had passed under triumphal arches to the acclaim of his fellow Americans. Now, as his barge approached the wharf, the boom of guns mingled with the cheering of the crowds along New York's shore.

French and Spanish warships joined the people in saluting the first head of a new nation—a new kind of nation "without nobles and without a king." It was a proud moment for New York City, as well as for all the "United States of America," so recently named.

This was the morning of April 23, 1789. A brightly decorated barge, rowed by thirteen ship captains, had just brought George Washington to his inaugural. For a week, the city was wild with excitement. From Hudson River towns, from distant communities in New England, and from states to the south, people had arrived on foot, by boat, by wagon, or on horseback to attend the thrilling event. At night the glare of bonfires and the shouts of revelers expressed a nation's joy.

Then came the day. The crowd was hushed as Washington appeared on the balcony of the City Hall. Placing his hand on the Bible, he repeated the oath of office slowly and emphatically: "I do solemnly swear that I will faithfully execute the office of President of the United States, and will to the best of my ability, preserve, protect and defend the Constitution of the United States, so help me God."

Instantly the new flag was raised. "Long live George Washington, President of the United States," roared the crowd. Then a humble and embarrassed Washington left the balcony to address the Congress.

For eight years the austere Washington presided over a Government that was praised by Europeans as "the most free one we know of . . . stronger, because juster, than any we witness in the Old [World]."

The America undertaking this democratic experiment was already a mixture of many peoples, although most were of British stock. It was a nation in which the poverty that haunted the rest of the world was largely absent. And there was none of the abject cringing so characteristic of the common man elsewhere. Americans believed strongly in equality. They disliked the word "servant," preferring "hired man" or "hired girl." When a hired man was asked if his master were home, the reply was sharp: "Master! I have no master. Do you want Mr. ——?"

Americans were proud of their country's vigor and its influence in the world. They owned a million square miles of "the forest primeval," which gave promise of great national power. It quickened the optimistic belief that the future could be made to come today.

But it took more than optimism to launch the new Government and turn it into a going enterprise. Fortunately, the people had their initial experience in self-government during the Colonial and Revolutionary years. The distinguished leadership of Washington, Hamilton, Adams, Jefferson, and Madison provided a Government with a firm foundation. On it was built a structure of enduring strength.

It was not easy. Alexander Hamilton had worked out a program to promote manufactures and establish a sound currency, but to do this required unpopular taxes. Farmers in Pennsylvania were so resentful that they staged the famous "Whisky Rebellion," in protest. Although the Government prevailed, submission of rebellious farmers did not mean acceptance of the Federalist program. Opponents formed the Republican party, led by Jefferson and Madison. These leaders believed that Hamilton's policies

concentrated too much power in the national Government and lessened the authority of the states. They charged the Federalists with aiding businessmen at the expense of the farmers.

Out of these different ideas of what the Government should do ultimately came two principal parties. Party history falls into three periods: Federalists against Republicans (1789-1816), Whigs against Democrats (1830-1856), and Republicans against Democrats (1856 to date).

The Federalists believed with Hamilton that "all communities divide themselves into the few and the many. The first are the rich and well-born, the other the mass of the people." They said the masses were "turbulent" and needed to be reined in by their betters.

But the mass of men would not be reined in. Led by Jefferson and Madison, they ousted the Federalists from the national Government in 1800 in an election that was spoken of as a "revolution." Against the gold braid and brass buttons of the Federalists, the Jeffersonians preached simplicity. Jefferson and his followers sincerely believed that the country had been rescued from an aristocratic clique. For the next twenty-eight years, to 1829, the country chose Republican Presidents: Jefferson, Madison, Monroe and John Quincy Adams. The Federalist party paid for its mistrust of the ordinary citizen; it slowly died.

Jefferson, author of the Declaration of Independence, expressed American ideals eloquently. The lanky Virginian, although a patrician in his tastes, had unbounded faith in democracy and embraced whole-heartedly the aspirations of common humanity. The people, he said, should be their own masters. Opposed to strong government, Jefferson urged as little interference as possible. People, he said, should be left "free to regulate their own pursuits of industry and improvement."

Nonetheless, Jefferson did not hesitate to use his executive power when the opportunity arose to buy the Louisiana territory from Napoleon. For

Territorial Expansion of the United States:
1. The thirteen original states.
2. First westward movement occupied area acquired by treaty with British in 1783. Settlers used Boone's Wilderness Road or the National Road through the Ohio Valley.
3. Big leap to Pacific Coast came in 1840's and 1850's and was spurred by gold strikes. Santa Fe, California, and Oregon were main trails across the plains. 4. Vast central area was the last to be settled. Homestead Act, railroads, and the opening of Oklahoma Territory and Cherokee Strip were major events that filled in the land.

11

four cents an acre, an immense region—the Louisiana Purchase—was acquired which extended the country's boundaries to the Rocky Mountains, to Canada and the Gulf.

Jefferson had little trouble making up his mind to buy it. Like most Americans he was an ardent expansionist. In Madison's time, expansionists also clamored for Canada and the pressure of western "War Hawks" on the President was severe. By 1812, England's interference with American shipping led to war. The conflict did not settle the rights of neutrals, nor did it win Canada for the United States. But it made Americans proud of their naval prowess and it gave the country another idol: Andrew Jackson, victor at New Orleans. Forgetting earlier defeats, Americans now boasted that "one Yankee could lick any ten foreigners." In 1819, Spain ceded Florida; the entire Atlantic seaboard was now free of foreign domination.

The men who had guided the country through the Revolution and its first perilous years of independence were dying. Jefferson and John Adams went together, on July 4, 1826. Their bequest was a nationalism that knew neither sectional boundaries nor differing philosophies of government. The country was, however, undergoing some important changes that strained national ties. Among the obvious ones were the spread of the cotton kingdom into the Southwest, the industrial revolution in eastern factory towns, and the rapid growth of the West. The seaboard states were faced with the challenge of new territories admitted to the Union: Kentucky in 1792, Tennessee four years later, Ohio in 1803, Louisiana in 1812, Indiana in 1816, Mississippi a year later, Illinois the year after that, Alabama in 1819, and Missouri in 1821.

In this vast, western region, especially in its northerly parts, there was established a type of society new to man's history. Tough pioneers had crossed mountains, ousted the Indians, leveled the forests, built cabins and houses. The land yielded the farmer and his family a rude but independent existence. In this setting, where life was about the same for everybody and where almost every adult, white male could vote, the political ideas of Jefferson seemed to have been realized. In this relatively simple society, government was an uncomplicated affair. Any able man could fill the office of sheriff, road supervisor, county clerk—even governor. "Ours is a country," said a proud American, "where men start from an humble origin . . . and where they can attain to the most elevated positions, or acquire a large amount of wealth, according to the pursuits they elect for themselves. . . . This is a country of self-made men, than which nothing better could be said of any state of society."

A pioneer wrote that his comrades were men of destiny. They may well have been, but the thought did not rest heavy upon them. They made the wilderness ring with music and laughter. Singing and shouting eased the tension that came from constant danger. They bragged to boost their courage; and they roared to shatter the deafening silence. Men delighted in practical jokes; the tall story told with a straight face amused one's fellows. The quirky humor of the frontiersman was copied by stage folk. Sam Slick, dressed up in Uncle Sam's red, white, and blue costume and speaking with a drawl, was a favorite at home and abroad. He told an English audience: "We Yankees don't do things like you Britishers; we are born in a hurry, educated at full speed, our spirit is at high pressure, and our life resembles a shooting star, 'til death surprises us. . . ."

In his growing community the pioneer was a booster, a gambler always betting on the future. Unlike the earlier fur trader or hunter, the farmer changed the face of the land. He had come to stay—at least for a while.

The dedicated minuteman, when his job was done, often became the dedicated pioneer.

The house he built was temporary because he expected soon to build a better one. While he tamed the land, the influence of women folk brought civilization to his environment. Child bearing, incessant work, and trying to hold the family together while restless husbands kept them on the move, wore wives down. The land was full of widowers. But the women, as long as there was life in them, spoke up against slavery and heavy drinking, and they fought for the education of their children.

The West, north of the Ohio, was largely without slavery. Farther South great changes were taking place, thanks to the cotton gin and newly invented textile machinery. As the demand for cotton increased sharply, more and more land was put under cultivation. Plantations took on the impersonal character of big business enterprises. Slavery was now said to be "a positive good."

The East was being altered, too. Its industries, favored by tariff protection, grew rapidly. The power of steam, applied to ship, railroad, and factory, overcame discouraging obstacles to progress and transformed hamlets into manufacturing centers. Immigration from Europe mounted and a high proportion of these newcomers stayed in Eastern cities. Only a hundred thousand foreign-born were in the country in 1830, when the total population was thirteen million. In the next twenty years, two-and-a-half million aliens entered the nation's lifestream.

The changed political alignment of the Jacksonian period saw the large-scale financiers and industrialists of the East opposed by urban workers, western farmers, southern slave owners—and newly naturalized immigrants. These diverse groups found their spokesman in gaunt Andrew Jackson, triumphantly elected in 1828 and already a national folk hero. "It was a proud day for the people," exulted a supporter. "General Jackson is *their own* president." Another admirer said, "The day for the multitude has now dawned. . . . It is now for the yeomanry and the mechanics to march at the head of civilization."

March they did, to the left. The very name of the Republican party was changed to Democrat, which seemed better suited to Jacksonian sentiments. The Democratic party was dedicated to a fight against monopoly and aristocracy. Small business men found its policies congenial, especially when aimed at the "Monster," the Bank of the United States.

The leftward swing in Jackson's party was characteristic of its western and northern supporters, not of those in the South. There resentment was growing against the President's strong nationalism and his eagerness to chastise South Carolina when it attempted to nullify a Congressional tariff measure. In a dramatic episode at a memorial dinner to Jefferson, Jackson rose, and looking straight at Vice President John C. Calhoun, of South Carolina, proposed the toast: "Our Union: it must be preserved."

This devotion to the Union was echoed by countless eloquent lawyers and politicians who were founders of the free commonwealths which filled the Mississippi Valley within two short generations. And by such as the spellbinding Daniel Webster, who cried, "Liberty *and* Union, now and forever, one and inseparable."

While Webster and others endorsed Jackson's nationalism, they opposed nearly everything else he favored. Discontented westerners, wanting more Government support for internal improvements, eastern manufacturers asking tariff protection, and southern antagonists of the President were welded together into the Whig party by Henry Clay. They chose William Henry Harrison as their candidate in 1840. Old Tippecanoe (he was a soldier and had won a battle against Indians there) "and Tyler, too" triumphed after a rollicking campaign, but Harrison died a month after his inauguration, and the Whigs would win only one more election—in 1848—with another military man, Zachary Taylor. The Democrats won all the other presidential elections in the period from 1828 to 1860. Now largely under southern direction, the Democrats sensed more acutely than did the Whigs the country's "Manifest Destiny" to spread southwest to Texas, westward to California, northwest to Oregon.

Southern states, in particular, were sending their sons and daughters to Texas. The territory was under Mexican rule, but would not remain so for long, once the Texans raised the Lone Star flag and began to agitate for independence. Shouting, "Remember the Alamo," Texans crushed the Mexicans in the battle of San Jacinto, and Winfield Scott's forces eventually marched overland from Vera Cruz to take Mexico City and end the war. Mexico lost not only Texas, but also New Mexico, Arizona, and California.

While Texas was a magnet for people east of the Mississippi and Utah attracted the Mormons, much of the region acquired from Mexico did not arouse great interest. The situation changed suddenly and dramatically when the glittering stuff in John Sutter's millrace in the Sacramento Valley turned out to be gold. From the ends of the earth, prospectors came, boosting California's small population enormously.

California asked to be admitted to the Union as a free state. This meant trouble. It seriously threatened the country's unity, expressed in its motto "E Pluribus Unum." Although peril was averted by compromise, slavery and other problems drove a wedge between the states north and south of Mason and Dixon's line. A new party arose, taking an old name— "Republican"—and appealed to those opposing the extension of slavery and to those in favor of free distribution of lands in the West.

The name Republican also recalled the ideals of Jefferson. Said a practical politician, "It is the cherished name with our foreign population of every nationality." Among its recruits was an Illinois lawyer, Abraham Lincoln. In 1858 he made a national reputation in a series of debates with Senator Stephen A. Douglas. In a shrill, penetrating voice, he told a listening country that slavery was a great moral wrong. Two years later at the Republican convention, ten thousand people screamed their support of the tall "Rail Splitter." His neighbors in Springfield, Illinois, sang and cheered through the night when the election returns came in.

Within a few months of his election, the President was faced with the agony of civil war. Three quarters of a century earlier the Revolution had given birth to a new nation. In this second war that nation almost committed suicide. Lincoln's genius saved it; the country remained the *United* States. In his immortal address at Gettysburg, he expressed the determination that America should remain a beacon of freedom to men everywhere.

When Johnny came marching home in the North, he was soon working again in the expanding cities and on the increased farm acreage of America's West. In the South, Johnny returned to find that the old plantation life was finished. Cotton was still king, but for some years the realm was poverty-stricken and disorganized. The road to reunion between North and South was slow and tortuous. While slaves were free, southerners and northerners alike were suddenly forced to adjust to an emancipated Negro.

In the North, too, farming underwent a revolution during the Civil War and in the reconstruction years that followed. On western grass, vast herds grazed and the fattened cattle were sent east to supply meat for fast-growing

The small town, the farm, the
big city—these were the places where most
Americans lived and worked. And the
Great Mississippi Steamboat
Race typified the competitive spirit that
spurred Americans everywhere.

cities. Cattlemen, homesteaders, and miners invaded Indian lands. The red men fought back, but the odds were hopeless. Chief Joseph of the Nez Percé spoke the final heartbreak of his people: "I am tired of fighting. Our chiefs are killed. . . . It is cold and we have no blankets. The little children are freezing to death. . . . My heart is sick and sad. From where the sun now stands, I will fight no more, forever."

Over the wide land were stretched the lengthening tracks of railroads. Forests yielded their giant trees, while the earth's interior supplied the coal and iron ore that made the nation first among industrial powers. Factories multiplied and cities grew with frantic speed.

The New World's strength had been built up in large measure by the help of immigrants who came because "they say there is work and bread for all." They came, too, because of religious liberty, free education, and the suffrage that made them active citizens in the community. A country requiring no passports was surely the land of the free.

From 1860 to 1912, all the Presidents, with the exception of Grover Cleveland, were Republicans. The party that had won with Lincoln now traded on his name in the freebooting 1870's to advance policies that gave free rein to big business. Big it was, indeed, for this was the period when many of the huge industrial complexes of today had their birth. The activities of industry's captains made the nation economically powerful, but they were a rigorous crew that brooked no opposition. Immense timber and mineral resources were given over to private enterprises. In Washington, in state capitols, and in city halls, political corruption was widespread.

The Republicans, riding high, derided the Democrats and marshaled their vote from Civil War veterans and farmers, many of whom were grateful for the virtually free land they had received under the Homestead Act of 1862. In time, however, the farmers felt less kindly toward their party, which was also the party of the railroads and corporations that were mistreating them.

Actually, the Democrats were little better. They gained in strength until national elections were being won by the margin of a few thousand votes. But neither party seemed truly interested in the ordinary man.

Angry farmers, tired of the politician's praise before election and neglect afterward, organized third parties, which won support from many people in the cities. The Populists made a good showing in 1892, and the Progressives, led by the fighting Theodore Roosevelt, did even better in 1912. But third parties seemed to have no future. It was simpler to take over one of the major parties. This was done when Bryan's "silver tongue" lifted the Democratic delegates out of their seats in 1896 and won him the presidential nomination. Although he lost in one of the most exciting elections in American history, he taught both parties that in the future they would have to heed progressive ideas.

Distraction from domestic politics came in 1898 in the war with Spain. The slogan "Remember the Maine" brought recruits from the city and cowboys from the plains to join Teddy Roosevelt's "Rough Riders" to fight in Cuba. Others sailed with Admiral Dewey to Manila Bay.

The war was quickly over, but America was not the same thereafter. It became more conscious of the outer world as the world became more aware of it. Lands beyond the traditional continental boundaries—Puerto Rico, Hawaii, and the Philippines—were added to the nation. The building of the Panama Canal began a new era for the country in world affairs.

At home, much of an earlier America remained. The pace of most of the nation was still geared to that of the horse. In the South, the small farmer was scarcely aware of the world beyond his acres and his isolated community. He labored to raise enough cotton to wind up the year in the black. It was the visits of drummers selling dry goods, hardware, harness, and other items that relieved the monotony of rural existence.

The Government in Washington still seemed remote; the post office was practically the only tie the individual had with it. Not that Americans were uninterested in politics. Quite the reverse. Politics was everybody's business. Banners fluttered along Main Street, and every farmhouse proclaimed its party loyalty. In every tavern, crossroads store, and town meeting, candidates and issues were hotly debated. Partisanship was intense. "Iowa will go Democratic when hell goes Methodist," shouted an orator.

Industry and thrift were prime virtues. Children grew to maturity repeating the lesson: "A Stitch in Time Saves Nine." Although thrift for individuals ("a penny saved is a penny earned") was preached, the nation's vast resources were squandered in the hurry to grow. It was a society that gloried in competition, often ruthless, but it was sentimental and had compassion for the defeated. This people of plenty were proud of their abundance, which they shared generously with victims of misfortune. American philanthropy was on a scale unprecedented in world history. Although the gap between rich and poor grew greater in the course of the Nineteenth Century, there was no hostility to wealth as such; the anger was against "malefactors of great wealth."

In their best moments, Americans remembered the principles on which the nation was founded; in their worst, their conscience pricked them for failing to live up to these ideals. They were a people whose greeting "Howdy, Stranger," was hospitable, not hostile. Although they were "rugged individualists," they were "joiners" of innumerable organizations. They could be severely critical of one another and make disparaging remarks about other countries, but resented criticism of America. They were skeptical ("I'm from Missouri"), but could be sold almost anything in the name of progress. Although they were involved in several wars and elected generals president, they were not a warlike people. Their instinct was anti-militarist; civilian authority was supreme. This principle was firmly fixed in the American grain by tradition and by the revered Constitution.

This book is about these Americans. It is not concerned with their role in the great national events outlined in this introduction; that is political history, known and familiar. Rather, it is the story of the daily life of the ancestors of all of us, from the inauguration of George Washington to the outbreak of World War I. It details the life of the country, the town, and the city, for these are the places in which all Americans have lived. And it seeks to show the common heritage of effort and optimism, of imagination and resolution, of courage and devotion that shaped these people's lives and helped give meaning and value to our own time.

In the Eighteenth Century, at a time when most of America was a wilderness, a prophecy was made:

"The Residence of Wild Beasts will be broken up . . . and the inestimable Treasures of Gold & Silver [will] be broken up. Huge Mountains of Iron Ore . . . will employ Millions of Hands, not only to form the martial Sword and peaceful Share . . . but an Infinity of Utensils . . . Stones from the vast quarries will be piled into great Cities. O! Ye unborn Inhabitants, when your Eyes behold the Sun after he has rolled the Seasons round for two or three Centuries more, you will know that we dreamed of your Times."

This is a family album of the people who made it happen.

19

The COU

When George Washington bade farewell to his troops, most of them went back to the farm. Some returned to the small, elegant cities now thriving under the stimulation of culture and commerce, and a few found their way back to the salty port towns. But for the majority, home was the land.

Land the new nation had in abundance. It was as limitless and rich in promise as the liberty on which the people now prepared to build—and, for the moment, as little realized. The United States reached from the Atlantic to the Mississippi and from the Great Lakes to Spanish Florida. It covered more than a million square miles and was larger than Europe. But most of the four million Americans lived on the eastern seaboard, at most a hundred miles inland from the beachheads their forefathers had established in the Seventeenth Century.

Even here, silent forests and untouched, sunlit fields separated the random settlements, and farms became cultivable only by unremitting labor against the encroachments of nature. What lay beyond was sensed rather than known. Only dour trappers, wily gun-runners, Indian traders, surveyors, and soldiers garrisoned in wilderness outposts—the restless ones who guard civilization's borders and scout the course ahead—had felt the immensity of the waiting land and looked westward toward the source of the winds. Only they had crossed the old trails of Spanish adventurers and French priests and could confirm the two-hundred-year-old accounts of what they had discovered.

In time the few would be followed by many, and eventually the pressure westward would become inexorable. Then the land would yield up its secrets and its opportunities, and the nation would realize its destiny.

But in New England in the first decades after the Revolution descendants of the original English settlers still worked hard to raise crops on their small farms. The fences marking the boundaries of their hundred acres were made of rocks or tree stumps dug from the land to clear it for the plow. Zig-zag fences were made of the trees that had been chopped down to allow the sun to reach the seed rows. Despite all the labor that the original owners had put into those farms, the men who inherited them were still working "from daybreak to backbreak." But, with the help of his wife and family, and when necessary a "hired man," a farmer could make his fields and skimpy pasture yield enough to feed them all and still have enough left to exchange at the crossroads store for things his farm could not produce.

"The most valuable crop a Connecticut farmer can raise," it was said, "is seven stalwart sons."

In the Connecticut Valley, the flatness and fertility of the land contrasted markedly with the slanting, boulder-strewn hills farther north that winded man and horse. Near Long Island, farmers went seining—paying out long

America had achieved her independence
and inaugurated her first President—himself a farmer—with
joyful ceremony. Now it was time for the soldier
to return to his hard-won fields. It was a time for growth and
development. The country must be made to
produce and thrive, new frontiers must be opened. After the
celebrations were over, there was work to be done.

Even within the relatively small area the early
settlers knew, the variety of the land was wide. Heavy forest covered much
of the country, so water provided the best transportation.

nets in the bounteous sea and drawing them back filled with whitefish to spread on their fields as fertilizer. This was a trick they had learned from the Indians and their reward was forty bushels of rye to the acre, along with handsome crops of corn and potatoes. But the hillsides of New England were less advantaged. The topsoil was too easily washed away and the earth, inadequately fertilized, became exhausted. Here prayers and fasting encouraged rectitude and sustenance was sought in the Bible.

Raising crops and tending cattle were only two of the farmer's endless tasks. He was likely to be his own carpenter, cooper, veterinarian, and blacksmith. Shoes for the family, made from the hide of his animals, were his own handiwork—sturdy, if not comfortable. (Left and right were the same. To tortured feet was given the job of stretching the shoes to a comfortable shape.)

Since hard money was scarce and paper money not always reliable, the farmer hoarded his small supply of coins and bought nothing he could possibly make for himself or do without. For example, corn could be ground on the farm, but wheat had to be milled. (The miller would accept wheat in payment for his labor, however.) Even when the farmer sold his butter, eggs, potash, feathers, and beeswax he did not receive cash, only "store pay" —credit to buy things at the country store. The store was the only commercial institution he trusted. He was suspicious of bankers and business men. *The New England Farmer* warned him to "shun the door of a bank as he would an approach of the plague or cholera."

A farmer bought iron, gunpowder and shot, occasionally some glassware or crockery or an imported piece of dress goods for fancy, and, for the table, sugar, salt, rum, molasses, tea, and coffee. To the coffee he added home-grown chicory. The purple paper that wrapped the ten-pound cone of sugar—a year's supply—was saved and used for dyeing cloth, thus avoiding an expenditure on costly indigo. One thrifty farmer boasted that, except for $10 worth of salt and iron, his farm supplied everything he needed.

No one would think of buying food. Farm diets were simple, but the

caloric intake was ample: "bean porridge hot, bean porridge cold," brown bread, hominy with milk, pork, salt beef, fish, vegetables, and fruit. When wheat was scarce, "rye and Injun" (maize) made the bread. Meat or fish might be served at every meal depending on the luck of the hunt or the catch. Puddings of maize or buckwheat were eaten at noonday dinners. Barrels of corned beef and salt pork were stored in the cellar, along with cheeses and crocks of pickles and preserves, against the long winter, and strings of dried fruits and vegetables hung in the attic.

Still, the farmer rarely ran to fat. The ritual of work filled fourteen hours of every day, beginning with the crowing of the cock at dawn. Even with the harvest reaped, there was little relief from the endless round of chores. The short autumn days were spent threshing, chopping wood, splitting staves and shingles, mending fences, and repairing tools. On gray winter mornings, when the breath hung frosty on the air, there was ice to be sawed at the pond and stored in sawdust and woodshavings in the icehouse, snow to be shoveled, or, when the roads were hard-packed with snow, logs to be hauled. In spare moments, agile hands occupied themselves with whittling. Spoons and bowls, a decoy duck, a comb, a pie-crust edger—all emerged from the well-cured wood, and sometimes the sharp, inventive mind created a labor-saving gadget. This was Yankee ingenuity, and soon one of the busiest departments of the young Government would be the Patent Office. "That's what comes from whittlin'," people said, admiringly.

Many of the inventions aimed at lightening the work of the women, who were no less busy than the men. New England women worked in the fields only at harvest time, but there was always more than enough to be done around the house.

By firelight the farm wife carded and spun the wool sheared from the sheep. The yarn was knitted into stockings, mittens, and shawls. She made homespun cloth to provide household linens and sacks for grain. Clothes were her own doing, too, even to her husband's breeches and jacket. Store-boughten finery, such as shoe buckles or a beaver hat or the broadcloth that went into a man's holiday coat, was very special. So was the imported silk for her best dress. Worn clothes were cut down for the young ones and eventually ripped into strips to be loomed or braided into rag rugs.

Wool was mixed with the linen produced from home-grown flax and made into linsey-woolsey. Cloth was also made by combining linen and cotton, or cotton and wool. Spinning wheel and loom were never idle for long. The housewife bleached the cloth and colored it with dyes extracted from wild flowers and the bark of butternut, hickory, and sassafras trees.

It was a woman's job to tend the kitchen garden, feed the chickens twice a day, and gather the eggs. Egg money was understood to be hers to spend as she wished at the crossroads store. Cooking and baking for her husband, children, and the hired man was her pride. "Settin' a good table," she called it. Washing, cleaning, preserving, and pickling were in her province as was the making of cheese, lard, candles, soap, and the churning of butter.

She also doctored members of the family or neighbors, even the animals. She knew which herbs made what medicines. Tansy and savory were blended with others in the mortar for spring remedies. She reminded everybody to take sulphur and molasses to purify the blood, sassafras tea to thin the blood. For a cold she wrapped the throat with a stocking soaked in goose grease.

Children were seldom idle. Boys fetched the cows; they chopped kindling wood and brought water from the well. As soon as they were big enough, they helped with the plowing and haying. On Saturday a boy helped his

Tools were primitive and
methods of farming simple. The most important
commodity was manpower. Even with
his whole family working and the occasional
help of a hired hand, it was a struggle for
the farmer to make his fields
yield sufficient food—and some left
over to trade at the store.

To ease the loneliness of farm life,
chores could be turned into occasions. Neighbors gathered to help
separate the flax, and the harvest was a happy event.

28

mother prepare the codfish cakes for Sunday's breakfast, so the family wouldn't be delayed for church. He ground the fish that had been soaked overnight. Despite the soaking it was still difficult to put through the grinder. It was a pleasure to put the cooked potatoes through when the last of the fish had been ground. Mother fried the fish cakes in the morning, along with the slices of corn-meal mush that would be served with maple syrup.

Girls weeded the garden and made a scarecrow to guard it. This was fun. It was no fun to scrub the kitchen, but they did it. They braided and sewed straw hats for the men, and the samplers they stitched adorned the walls.

Even the dog did his share, keeping an eye on the cows, sheep, and pigs. He might be put to running on a treadmill that pumped a butter churn. And he kept the farmer company during the tedious business of plowing, following alongside horse or oxen, just as the cat followed the farmer's wife at milking time.

The Sabbath was a day of rest—relatively. All that had to be done was to milk and pasture the cows, water the horses, feed the hens and pigs—and attend church for most of the day. It took time, too, to dress in one's Sunday best, but father always made up a few minutes racing his buggy against the others on the road to church.

Church seats were hard almost beyond endurance. Bringing your own armrest helped ease the strain, but nothing could shorten the sermons. In winter there was additional discomfort, for the church was unheated. The little foot warmer fought the chill, but had to be refilled frequently with live coals from the Sabbaday House. After church, of course, the nearby tavern was ready to dispense a potion that would keep a body from freezing.

For men, the rigorous farm life was eased a little during the few days spent each year in militia training. "Muster days" were a rollicking time, with music and hard cider, much "rasslin'" and rough-and-tumble horseplay. Soldiering seemed a minor consideration. In season, men played quoits or bowls, and sailed their small boats in New England's waters. From boyhood youngsters skated, fished, and hunted; they also played football with an inflated pig's bladder.

For women, there were the quilting bees, as well as apple-peeling parties at apple-butter time. These usually were festive occasions, with refreshments. Everybody liked cornhuskings. Gathered in a neighbor's barn, they chose sides and began stripping the ears. "The yells of defiance," one account says, "reverberated . . . through the woods, whilst an increasing shower of corn streamed through the air." The gaiety increased when some one uncovered a red ear of corn and won the right to kiss a girl.

When husking was finished and the floor finally swept clean, the dancing began. The fiddler, who also served as caller, urged the folks to jig, "cut the pigeon wing," and finally to let go and "cut the double shuffle." The dancers jumped in the air, clicking their heels, while bystanders encouraged them on with cheers and laughter.

In stern communities where the barn dance was considered sinful, a "frolic" took its place. If there were moonlight the party might be held out of doors. The little brown jug was counted on to thaw the bashfulness of a young man, so he would be ready to offer a girl his arm and start the marching. At the command to "open a ring," all took hands to encircle one person, who then chose a partner. Everyone sang:

Green grow the rushes, O!
Kiss her quick and let her go!
But don't muss her ruffle, O!

There were various "marching plays" with much bowing, kneeling, and skipping to the accompaniment of a song. There were many games involving the forfeit of a kiss, so these frolics were also knows as "bussing" bees. One of the most popular songs was the "Weevily Wheat" song that included the stanza:

> *The higher up the cherry tree*
> *The sweeter grows the cherry,*
> *The more you hug and kiss a gal*
> *The more she wants t' marry!*

In winter a young man did his courting beside the fire in the girl's home—after the small children had been sent to bed and the parents at length found excuses to absent themselves.

Often enough, life on the farm was hard. But it had many charms that were recalled most clearly as the moment came to leave. "When the land is impoverished," a discouraged farmer wrote, "one goes off to Kentucky or the Genesee." Cutting the ties was never easy, but leached-out soil and thin harvests usually forced the decision. The oxcart was drawn up before the house and all that could be carried was stowed aboard. There was never enough room for everything. Choosing what to take and deciding what could be left behind caused many heartaches. Tools had top priority; they would make the new life possible. A crate of poultry was essential to perpetuate the flock, and perhaps a pair of shoats. The larger stock would walk, tethered behind the cart. The clothes chests that stood at the foot of each bed would be taken. And seed, dried foods, cooking utensils, and the Bible. Intimate, indoor elements of the home, they now sat nakedly exposed.

The children welcomed the new venture. Only later would their thoughts go back to the brook, the haymow, the sheltering barn, the paths to familiar places, the sights and sounds of home. The dog, knowing something was up, scampered aimlessly.

For New Englanders, the Genesee was often the first objective. The word was that the route to western New York was fairly level; some ups and downs, but no mountains to traverse. They would cross the Hudson River at Troy, or perhaps Newburgh or Catskill. Taxes were said to be fairly low and the people were mostly your own kind. They built much the same kind of home—the well-off painted theirs white, with green shutters —even to the steeply pitched roof to shed the snow. It was a comforting prospect. The family's hopes were high.

In the 1780's, more than 100,000 people took to the road in search of better land. Many were veterans of the war, off to claim the free acreage promised by a grateful Government. Southerners went to the Cumberland Valley, following Daniel Boone and the "Long Hunters" who, pursuing

Although there was little relief from
the farmer's seemingly endless daily tasks, he sometimes found
a moment to sit by his fire and
whittle, a pleasant—and useful—pastime. In such
quiet interludes, a child might hear stories
of how the Revolution was won.

the forest trail of bison seeking salt, had found the Gap and opened the Wilderness Road. The Road was no more than a pack trail at first, winding through dense woods, climbing innumerable ridges, and crossing cold mountain streams.

Pioneers heading west from Philadelphia reached Kaintuck by a different route. They trekked for three hundred miles over the mountains of Pennsylvania to the Monongahela River, where they waited at Pittsburgh to board rafts that floated down the Ohio.

These flatboats were partly roofed-over and their freeboard rose like a battlement, affording some protection when Indian arrows began to fly from the shore. The families and their livestock were crowded aboard. The boats edged into the current and floated downstream. They traveled as a flotilla, a cumbersome herd, clustering against danger. Companionship was important, not only for the safety it brought, but for the consolation, as well. For smallpox and malaria were as deadly as the redskin, and bereaved families often were taken in by their new-found friends of the river.

The pioneers who went to the Cumberland region found rocky ridges and fertile bottom-lands in the deep, narrow, crescent-shaped valley cut by the river. Some of the early settlers built their simple pole cabins in the rocky highlands. But the more enterprising sought the valley, where limestone and rich bluegrass were evidence of the earth's fertility. Here they built fine, double-log cabins with deep stone fireplaces.

In the two generations following the establishment of the Federal Government, Americans pushed to the west in ever-growing numbers. The caravans often were pitifully small: a little wagon pulled by two small horses or, if the travelers were less prosperous, a cart and single horse and the family plodding wearily alongside. The poorest pilgrim carried his belongings on

32

The ride to church—
perhaps on a "settled frost"—was but
part of a Sabbath nearly as
busy as the rest of the week.
Getting ready took time, church
took a lot more time, and there was
always the stock to tend.

The role of the farmer's
wife was no less important than his own.
She spun the thread, wove
the cloth, sewed the clothes. She kept a garden and
prepared all the food. The chickens
were hers to care for, but the
egg money was hers to keep. She also served
as a Sunday School teacher and even was
her own family doctor.

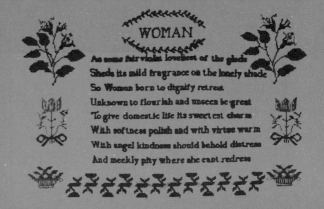

WOMAN

As some fair violet loveliest of the glade
Sheds its mild fragrance on the lonely shade
So Woman born to dignify retreat
Unknown to flourish and unseen be great
To give domestic life its sweetest charm
With softness polish and with virtue warm
With angel kindness should behold distress
And meekly pity where she cant redress

his back, followed by his wife "naked-footed, bending under the hopes of the family."

After settling on a homesite, the family built its cabin. With the help of neighbors, it was put together in a day and the goods that had been carried so far were moved in before sundown. As soon as possible, the newcomer planted corn and a truck patch was laid out for cabbage, beans, cucumbers, and potatoes. All growing things had to be protected from the raids of squirrels, crows, and rabbits. In Wisconsin, the gopher was a menace.

Most of the southerners who went west were small farmers who settled on three hundred acres and cleared ten. The swiftest way to remove trees was by girdling them and setting them on fire the following winter when they were dead and dried out. A "deadnin' " over several acres was a terrifying sight that reddened the night sky and reflected off the melting snow.

Birds and animals of the forest were shot for food. Deer, bear, and turkey were staple meats and squirrel broth was often on the menu. Bear and deer also supplied useful by-products: hides, grease, sinews. The family eagerly awaited the ripening of the corn so that it could once more enjoy corn-meal mush and hoe cakes. Wild honey was a great treat. The children trailed bees through the meadows to find the swarm. Pigeons, in flocks sometimes thirty miles long, filled the sky with the thunder of their flight and broke the overburdened branches of trees when they alighted.

For those who ventured into the flatlands of Ohio, Indiana, and Illinois, the fearful hazard was the prairie fire. Grass dried brittle by the summer sun blazed with incredible speed, blackening the sky with smoke and searing everything in its path—homes, livestock, occasionally a luckless settler.

The settler on the plains built himself a hut, open on the south side and heated by an outside cooking fire which also warned away the marauding

coyote. Bearskins and wolf pelts lined the walls to cut the wind and also served as beds.

His permanent home was not likely to be a vast improvement. It was of logs, with or without the bark, and often enclosed only a single room. A visitor to Ohio in 1821 was shocked by the crudeness of the "habitations" he saw. Even the judge, he discovered, lived in one room "in which all the family, with their guests, eat, sleep and perform all the domestic operations." The residence of a state senator contained but one room, with "a bed in two corners, in another a cupboard, in the fourth a swill-barrel, and on one side of the room a wooden clock without a case, and by one window a three-cornered piece of looking-glass."

The prairie land looked easy to work, but it was tough and stubborn. Heavy grass, as tall as a man astride a horse and with roots as thick as a thumb, made a sod no ordinary plow could cut. An acre could be bought for $1.25, but it cost three times as much to break the ground and fence it. In addition, a settler would need $250 for a span of horses, a double wagon, a yoke of oxen, a cow, various tools, and a plow—if he had been unable to bring them along. He shaped the handles of his tools from hickory, if he could find it. He also constructed his own beds, tables, stools, and chairs.

Men short of cash even made their own wagons. Wheels were circular slices of a large tree trunk. An Indiana woman wrote that when the wagon was finished, she and her father drove thirty-five miles to buy a plow. "After that," she said, "we didn't have to hoe up any more land."

It was a land of young people. An old man, even a gray hair, was uncommon. The call went out:

> Come all ye Yankee farmers who wish to change your lot,
> Who've spunk enough to travel beyond your native spot
> And leave behind the village where Pa and Ma do stay,
> Come follow me and settle in Michigania,
> Yea, yea, yea, in Michigania.

Frontier life was isolated, lonely, and brutally fatiguing. But a young man faced these difficulties with confidence when he loved a girl and undertook to build a home for her. Romantic love—marrying the girl of one's choice, without consideration of a dowry—was a cherished American custom. It was made possible simply because the young man could get land cheap and, by his own efforts, make a house for his bride, and raise food to feed a family.

The girl he loved might have some qualms about facing the hardships of the wilderness, but love could blind her to the well-known facts. And, besides, in her early teens she had begun to worry about remaining a spinster. The position of a maiden aunt was not an enviable one in any home.

A wedding in the West might find the bride dressed in linsey-woolsey and the groom in homespun, but the wedding feast would not be skimped. Preparing for it the family's womenfolk and neighbors spent busy days. The table, outdoors, was loaded with turkey and "stuffin'," pork and roast beef with gravy, a huge chicken pot-pie, and vegetables, pickles, and sauces, to say nothing of corn bread, crullers, custard, and pies. The poundcake was baked in coffee cups and iced with maple sugar. The tea or coffee was taken with or without "sweetnin'." Sweetnin' might be tree sweetnin', bee sweetnin', or sorghum.

To partake of this feast, the men and boys came first. The jokes were pungent and lively. After the old folks had gone home, the dancing began. The young couple dared not leave till midnight. Then their guests put them to bed and returned later to torment them with a "shivaree" outside their

Children worked—and
pauses in the long farm day were
few. Boys barely in
their teens were expected to
help with the plowing
and haying. There was a saying in
Connecticut that the
best crop a farmer could raise
was seven stalwart sons.

cabin. A wild banging and shouting were part of the terrible serenade, and the groom was beset by demands that he come out and offer drinks.

Settlers found the apparel that had served them well back East had a short life on the frontier. They quickly adopted the dress of the hunter and the Indian: coonskin cap, buckskin moccasins, dressed-skin breeches and shirt.

The West was a mixture of many peoples, and in time the language of the region was likewise a blend of accents and attitudes. Into it went much of the flavor of the Southern Appalachians. In his new home as in his old, the Southern Highlander "blowed," "knowed," "ketched," "was borned," he "heered" or "hearn say." In his nasal drawl he also spoke words he had made up: "shootin' iron," "lackbrain," "clutchfist." He enjoyed practical jokes and his humor had a special twist. To the frequent question, "Where does this road go?" he was likely to answer, "Don't go nowheres, Mister. Stays right there."

So it did. But wherever it led the people traveled. Gradually they populated the empty spaces. By 1803, there were enough of them to make a state of Ohio. Michigan became a territory in 1805, Illinois in 1809. In the South, the migration spread from the Carolinas across Indian country, through Tennessee, Georgia and Alabama, to Louisiana. By 1830, the perimeter of expansion ran in an arc from Detroit to New Orleans. It was not a smooth curve; it advanced where rivers and valleys made the going easy and was retarded when Indian opposition or natural obstacles were severe, or where a satisfactory terminus to the long march had been found.

By 1840, the line went from Green Bay to Corpus Christi and many of the indentations had been filled. As the Civil War approached, the boundary line was almost straight, from north to south, along the western edge of Iowa and Missouri.

Sometimes it appeared that the whole country was on the move. And, indeed, with half a continent stretching before them, the pioneers were free to wander as far as their inclinations and their stamina would take them. Yet their going did not depress the old settled areas of the thirteen original states. Their populations, too, were growing and thriving, and their social patterns becoming fixed.

South of the Ohio was a rural world quite different from that in the North. Its big crops were tobacco in Virginia and Kentucky, rice in Carolina and Georgia, sugar in Louisiana—and everywhere cotton. The land where cotton was king stretched a thousand miles from South Carolina to Texas.

Young lads from the towns that fringed

the rural areas could try their hands at trapping

a country rabbit; for farmers

the cornhusking bee was a seasonal rite. Everybody came.

Opposing teams were chosen and competition

was heated. After the husking, a moonlight frolic or a gay barn

dance was held. In either

case, the little brown jug was passed freely.

39

Before the Civil War, the South's leadership was in the hands of a thousand families, many of them related. The owner of a large plantation lived in a mansion whose slender columns were festooned with jasmine. It stood, graceful and imposing, at the head of a broad, graveled avenue, bordered by trees that formed a shady promenade. A semicircular flight of stairs led to a piazza, where vases of rose geranium perfumed the air. Holly and flowering shrubs lined the walks and fine saddle horses grazed on the lawn.

A procession of slaves moving from the separate kitchen building to the dining hall of the manse provided perfect service for the master's sumptuous three-o'clock dinner. His supper was served at dusk on the piazza. Tea and coffee were followed by brandy made from the plantation's peaches.

The conversation was often of politics, fine horses—and the price of cotton. At a fish fry, planters might gather to drink their whiskey near a well-shaded stream, eat soft-shell crabs, and talk of slaves, crops, and shooting matches. The ladies were invited only to the barbecue, which was more sedate. It was held under a specially built arbor, with many guests gathered to dance and indulge their appetites.

Southern hospitality was a deep-rooted tradition. A visitor might come "to week it, month it or summer it." A plantation owner would even order his servants to treat any passing traveler as a guest.

The relatively simple social life of Washington's day had become elaborate. Teas, balls, and visits followed each other in gay succession. John Tyler may have been more extravagant than most. For boating on the James River he had a bright blue boat with satin damask cushions. The slaves who rowed it wore blue-and-white uniforms and sky-blue hats, embroidered with his plantation's proud name, Sherwood Forest.

Owners of large plantations ordinarily divided their vast holdings into units of a thousand acres, each worked by a hundred slaves. Prime field hands, men and women just past twenty, were the choice workers and were recruited for the Deep South from Virginia, Kentucky, and eastern plantations.

The master and mistress might be kind, but the overseer often was not. His success was measured by the season's produce and he drove the slaves hard. Whipping was common. The slave's defenses were a slackened pace, theft, arson, flight, and sometimes revolt. Most slaves accepted, in resignation perhaps, this ancient abuse of man by man. Plaintive songs released the sorrow that burdened their hearts.

On a Louisiana plantation, the "rolling season" toward the end of October brought a time of merriment. The slave had harvested his own little crop,

When the soil was exhausted, the family had to pack its possessions on wagons and go in search of a new home, hopefully where the earth was good and not expensive. Free acreage was promised to veterans of the Revolution, and many from the South followed Daniel Boone's trail through the Cumberland Gap into Kentucky and Tennessee.

The nation began to sprawl westward.

he had received his winter clothes, and now, while sugar was being made, he was free to drink all the cane juice he wanted. Every available hand had been worked to cut the sugar cane, take it to the mill, and prepare a thousand cords of wood for boiling the juice. A Yankee visitor described the merry-making: "They dance and frolic as much as they please; and the cane song . . . now breaks night and day upon the ear, in notes 'most musical, most melancholy.'"

Between the four million slaves at the bottom and the few thousand whites at the top were other elements of the South's population. The great majority of southern whites held no slaves. They generally cultivated their acreage by themselves, although occasionally a few slaves worked side by side with the white yeomen.

On the lowest level of white society were the "poor whites." They were the inhabitants of Poverty Hollow, Scuffle Ridge, Scrabbletown, almost as barren of hope as the ground they walked, despised by the aristocracy and made listless by hookworm and malaria.

Temporary release from their troubles came at revival meetings when a "monstrous fine preacher" arrived to lift their spirits. The woods rang with the sermon. "He began low but soon bawled to deafening," a northern visitor said of a typical preacher. "He spit on his hands, rubbed them together. . . . The people now began to . . . dance and shout til they fairly drowned the speaker. . . . The sinners came tumbling down. . . ."

Mostly women and children were down. The young men took their hands to help them to their feet and assist them in the jumps that followed. Several feet in the air they leaped, hundreds of them at once, and all screamed, "Glory! Glory!" As exhaustion overtook ecstasy, they fell to the earth and

Pioneers heading west from Philadelphia took a
three-hundred-mile pack trip
over the mountains to Pittsburgh. There they boarded rafts that
floated down the Ohio. Many such arks drifted
along together and, as was always true of early caravans,
companionship was important. Help was
available if needed, and defense was stronger against attack.

44

rolled about, continuing their shouting till they were moved to approach the preacher and be prayed for.

A camp meeting was more decorous and might last for weeks. The preaching was long and solemn, the praying and singing incessant. Often the services were held by the light of huge bonfires. With the older folks occupied, the young ones managed to include some love-making on the side. For everyone excitement came in the baptismal ceremony, when the sinners waded into the water, the women's skirts ballooning, while the crowd on the banks of the creek sang "to outsing all music."

While religion played an important part in the lives of the lowly, the upper class was not too deeply concerned with it. A New England poet, visiting in Virginia in 1818, remarked that "the ancient Episcopal churches, which were once so prominent, are mostly in a state of dilapidation. The rank reeds rustle their doors; the fox looks out at their windows."

The lot of the small farmer in the older sections of the South grew worse when the large planters expanded their holdings. The yeomen moved west in covered wagons through the dust to Arkansas and Texas.

On the eve of the Civil War, Texas was growing more cotton than South Carolina. A generation earlier, John Randolph, gazing over deserted fields in Virginia, had already noted that "the old families are gone." But the rush could not be stemmed. In the South, as in the North, the West lured the adventurous and the discontented. Who could resist places like Ohio, where the earth needed "only to be tickled with the hoe to laugh with the harvest?"

Even before the land east of the Mississippi was well settled, Americans were hearing about more distant Edens in the Far West. The region had been explored by Lewis and Clark, Zebulon Pike, and the Mountain Men, who brought back exciting reports of the land's wonders. George Catlin had painted the Plains Indians, bringing to easterners vivid pictures of redmen, the buffalo they hunted and the wild horses they tamed.

New generations of Americans talked of going west. Reports of those who had gone to Oregon as missionaries to the Indians, and the spur of the depression after 1837, induced thousands to undertake the two-thousand-mile trek. They had worried that the treeless plains were a Great American Desert and that the Rocky Mountains were an impassable barrier. Jim Bridger and other mountain men knew that the Rockies were passable and they believed also in the land's fertility. A report to the government had said, "A man must know little of the American people who supposes that

When the settler had chosen his homesite, he built a

log cabin. With the help of

his neighbors, the simpler structures could be put up in

a day. The new farm usually consisted of about

three hundred wooded acres; the farmer

cleared ten and, as soon as possible, planted corn. While

waiting for it to come up, the family

depended for food on wild game in the forest.

Hunting and trapping provided the bear, deer, and turkey that were staples of the pioneer's diet. Bear and deer also supplied grease, sinews, and hides.

they can be stopped by anything in the shape of mountains, deserts, seas or rivers."

"Oregon fever" swept the country and Horace Greeley called it "an aspect of insanity." (When he said, "Go West, young man," he meant Ohio.) On the five-month migration westward, bugles gave the starting signal each morning and the column plodded on in platoons of four. Each day they changed positions, so that no one bore more than a fair share of tail-end dust.

Although guide books warned that wagon loads exceeding a ton could not make the mountain passes, many tried to make it with more and reached the sad moment when cherished possessions had to be abandoned. Women clung to the last to their silver, some decent Sunday clothes, some rose slips. They sobbed in the quiet darkness for the comforts of their old homes—and with reason. Fever and dysentery struck ruthlessly. Indians, broiling sun, violent line storms, and the overpowering vastness of the land bore heavily upon them.

Kentucky-born Jesse Applegate wrote in pride :"No other race of men . . . would undertake so great a journey—none save those could successfully perform it with no previous preparation, relying only on the fertility of their invention to devise the means to overcome each danger and difficulty as it arose. . . . The way lies over trackless wastes, wide and deep rivers, rugged and lofty mountains, and is beset with hostile savages. Yet . . . they are always found ready and equal to the occasion, and always conquerors. May we not call them men of destiny?"

Prairie schooners crossed the sea of grass and continued from the Platte River to Fort Laramie, over six hundred miles from their starting point at Independence, Missouri. At Laramie, wagons were repaired for the rough part of the journey northwestward across the Rockies. Weary, footsore animals had to have new shoes. Tender-footed oxen were sometimes given moccasins of raw buffalo skin.

Through South Pass, seventy-five hundred feet above sea level, the way was open to Fort Bridger, west of the Continental Divide. Jim Bridger, trapper and protector of emigrants, had built the fort as a supply station. Beyond was a canyon-like valley and then Fort Hall, on the Snake River. Hard mountain traveling still lay ahead before the easier path along the Columbia River was reached. The trial passed Fort Walla Walla and Fort Vancouver, and ended at last at Astoria or the Willamette Valley. In this new Canaan, most of the early Oregon pioneers put down their roots.

Along the Pacific Coast, Americans had been trapping otter for their skins since the end of the Eighteenth Century. They had also been busy with the "hide and tallow trade." California's ranches each year supplied thousands of hides for eastern shoe manufacturers and tallow for candles in South American mines. Ships from Atlantic ports rounded Cape Horn laden with sugar, coffee, hardware, clothing, shoes, furniture. The ships went up and down the Pacific Coast, anchoring in harbors, for all the world like floating department stores.

Trade, cattle raising, and fur trapping had brought about an increase in the American population in California even while it was a possession of Mexico. But the explosive event that changed the history of state and nation, and brought thousands of new settlers, was the discovery of gold.

In January, 1848, James Marshall, a mechanic working for John Sutter, the overlord of the Sacramento Valley, had found gold in a millrace. Marshall told only Sutter, and the two men sat on their secret for a few months. But it was too big to keep. Word leaked out, swept California, and flew eastward, the story improving with every mile. Outsiders longed to believe, but hated to be gullible. It sounded too much like another deceitful rumor spread by speculators to lure the unwary to California. In December of 1848, however, a Californian arrived in Washington with two-hundred-and-thirty ounces of pure gold. All doubt was dispelled. The stampede was on.

Americans were seized with madness. Farmers left their plows, preachers their pulpits, sailors their ships, and soldiers their posts. Through Panama's fever-ridden Isthmus, by ship around the Horn, or overland by covered wagon, the "forty-niners" converged on California. To the tune of "Oh, Susanna," they sang:

> Oh, California,
> That's the land for me:
> I'm off for Sacramento
> With my washbowl on my knee.

The washbowl, to be sure, had nothing to do with cleanliness. This was the only implement the dreamers felt they needed to scoop a fortune out of the mountain streams. In mid-May, 1848, five thousand wagons deepened the ruts of the California trail. A few weeks later, forty thousand men set out from Missouri, heading for the golden land.

Thousands never made it. These were the victims of illness, starvation, thirst, the freezing cold of the mountains, and their own pitiful ignorance and incompetence. Still they came, undeterred, wrapt in the vision, mistaking their optimism for resolution and courage.

The fever was contagious. "Limies" from London, "Coolies" from China, "Paddies" from Ireland, and "Keskydees" from France—"Qu'est-ce qu'il dit?" asked puzzled Frenchmen in a strange land. "What is it that he says?" —picked, shoveled, and panned for gold alongside native Americans. Crude communities sprang into being: Last Chance, Grub Gulch, Poker Flat, Flapjack Canyon, Hangtown. Here, in shacks and tents lining dusty streets, were the parasite necessities attending the boom: gambling halls, saloons, the

Nature and man often killed wantonly.
Although the Indian had long depended on the bison for his
livelihood, the herds continued to
flourish until the coming of the white man and the railroad. Then
a tragic and wasteful slaughter ensued. Nearly as
devastating was the terrifying sweep of the
prairie fire. Dry grass flaming at incredible speed blackened
and destroyed everything in its path.

assay and claims offices, the hardware store, and the grocery. By the end of '49, California's population had swelled to a hundred thousand.

For some the money came easy, for all the money went fast. Sugar was $4 a pound, flour $4 a barrel, whiskey $20 a quart. Truckmen made $25 a day. Eastern newspapers, months old, brought a dollar apiece. In a night men gambled away the gold that had cost them days of sweat. The average miner reaped no great riches. By the primitive hand methods he used, an ounce of gold, worth about $16, was a good day's work. Sitting by his fire, drinking his red whiskey from a tin can and smoking a rank cigar, the miner dreamed of a lucky strike. But the really successful mining was done by the big combines that had the resources to buy machinery and penetrate the mountains where the big veins lay.

The end of easy returns for the solitary miner sent him off with his mule and washing pan to search for other prospect. In 1858, toward summer's end, a prospector carried news to the outside world of gold found in the region of Pike's Peak. Again the gold bug bit. Farmers hit by the panic in 1857 joined the rush. Their pitchforks were a novel tool for prospecting in Cripple Creek, Colorado, which was called "the $300,000,000 cow pasture." A clerk in Iowa wrote: "It was all talk and dream, and yet . . . we were hotter about it than a prairie fire."

Thousands started out for the new diggings, painting on their covered wagons, "Pike's Peak or Bust." Many turned homeward "busted" for, with few exceptions, the lone prospector, like his brothers in California, found the competition too strong. Again it was machinery and engineering skill that made the big killings.

For the lucky few, spectacular strikes continued to be made, especially in silver. Horace Tabor made his fortune in Leadville. Others did so in Central City, once "the richest square mile on earth." One of the greatest strikes in history was made in Nevada, 1859. Lazy Henry Comstock, who gave his name to fabulous Comstock Lode, bluffed his way into sharing a lode discovered by others. The "black stuff" assayed $5,000 a ton in silver and $1,600 in gold. And another rush began. This time the hub was raffish Virginia City, which lived on hope and violence until, as always, the veins gave out.

While miners burrowed for riches, others sought their reward above ground. The western prairies and the Great Plains were the last areas to be tamed and brought under control by the white Americans. The foredoomed Indian tribes resisted. The warfare was cruel, and degraded by treachery, false promises, and shocking injustice on both sides. These dark deeds dimmed

Everyone had to have horses

to cover the vast stretches of ground. They had to be

purchased with cash and were valued highly

by farmers and cattlemen. The more affluent South, however,

could afford to use some of its

stock for sport. Blood lines and riding skills were

developed, and the hunt became

a typical diversion for the prosperous planter.

*While there were many rich
plantation owners, most of the southern farmers had
no slaves and very little property. A temporary
break in the field hands' labors came at camp-meeting time. The dramatic
preacher roared at his congregation, and the "sinners"
shouted and danced until exhausted.*

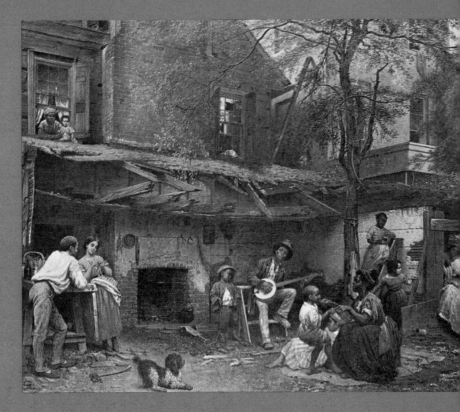

the glory of westward expansion and the painful paradox was that, however villainous the perpetrators of specific outrages, the conflict soon became so general that men of good will killed and were killed as readily as anyone else.

Yet taken by itself, the impulse to give productiveness and utility to the land, to knit the coasts together and consolidate the nation was a good one. It was undertaken with fervor and indomitable spirit. Anyone who stood in its way would have been a loser.

They were not all charmers, these nation builders. They had to be tough and they were. Tough men, tough women and children. Gentility fared poorly in pioneer accommodations. Arduous work and relentless weather creased and reddened the skin, calloused the palms, coarsened speech, and made for cross-grained personalities that could survive. Withal, they had a breadth of outlook. Their immediate goals might be simple—to find a decent piece of land, to raise a family, to live unhindered—and to achieve them they could stoop to meanness—by chiseling the Indian, by diverting water from a neighbor, by settling differences with force. But they had the courage to believe steadfastly in what a country of free men might be and they gave their strength willingly to make it happen. And from this sprang the bravado, the ebullience, the sweeping optimism, the funnin', the demon energy, the pulse and heartbeat whose vigor is felt to this day.

First arrivals on the plains staked out land along the streams where trees gave shelter to the animals and lumber for cabin, barn, and fences. Late-comers dug into the earth. With the tree clumps pre-empted, there was nothing to build with but sod. Settlers excavated a site and built walls of sod bricks around the rim. A ridgepole supported the branches that served as ceiling beams, and sod blocks were laid thickly on them to form a roof. Clay was troweled into crevices between the blocks. Greased paper was used in the windows and gunnysacking or buffalo hides hung in the doorway. The floor was earth, hard-packed. The "soddies" were wonderfully staunch. They withstood dust storms, and tornadoes rarely dislodged more than a few blocks that could be quickly repaired. Heavy rains made them leak mud, but after spring showers wildflower seeds sprouted in the sod and the walls and roof were bright with larkspur and columbine.

*The graceful homes of the
wealthy planters marked the top of
the South's leadership.
Entertainment at this level was lavish
and hospitality legendary. The
slaves were likely to
receive harsh treatment from their overseer,
but they managed to enjoy a little
merrymaking themselves. Plaintive songs
were often the release for
the sorrows that haunted their lives.*

54

The prosperity and serenity of the
country began to be disturbed by tormenting issues—
political, economic, and racial. Ordered
progress faltered and feelings were abraded by tension.
John Brown's raids and subsequent execution symbolized the violence of the
emotions that permitted the Civil War to happen.
Until it was over, national
development came to a virtual standstill.

Once he had gotten past
hostile ranchers and
warring Indians, the western farmer
had to contend with nature's
savage elements. In
spite of the hazards involved,
newcomers poured into the
prairie country and the open
grasslands were turned into
cultivated farmland.

Sod was fine natural insulation, as well. When the summer sun was so hot men "sweated dry salt," a soddy offered cool escape. In winter it was not difficult to heat.

Heavy crops of wheat and oats attracted men to the plains. The land, compared to flinty, grudging New England soil, was unbelievably fecund. Yet the growing season was full of hazard and the yield was brought to harvest at a cost. When rainfall was fickle, parched winds withered the grain and fruit was stricken on the branch. When rain was plentiful, floods threatened, and rain during a dust storm battered the waving wheat with pellets of mud. Biblical affliction came in the time of the locust. In clouds that hid the sun, they descended, wings whirring insanely, and devoured all that grew. Insatiably they consumed dry leaves, paper, textiles. They swarmed on a sheep's back, their mandibles snipping at the wool.

Tarred rags and ropes were fired and snaked along the ground to destroy the pest. Children earned bounty money with the buckets of locusts they killed. But these efforts were unavailing. Not until a region was barren did the plague depart.

Men defied the winds, floated on the floods, outlasted the locusts, repaired and replanted. Turkey-red, a strain of wheat introduced into Kansas in the 1870's by Russian Mennonites, proved resistant to the droughts that shriveled and stunted other varieties. Within twenty years, wheat growers from Oklahoma to Manitoba owed their livelihood to Turkey-red. Further, the outpourings of industry, now spreading to consumers everywhere, gave aid and comfort to the farmer. Cyrus McCormick's farm machines—harrows, reapers, and big threshers—were increasing the efficiency and productivity of every farmer who could afford them. This was a major factor in the ability of northern granaries to feed the Union effort in the Civil War.

The war was the first drastic break in the nation's zestful progress in a hundred years. Other wars had been fought. Panics and depressions had touched many homes. Great issues had been debated and resolved. But nothing like the Civil War had so divided Americans emotionally and philosophically. And when it came, its scythe swept clean. In rural areas throughout the nation, farms and fields were stripped of manpower. A visitor to Iowa reported seeing many women "driving teams, . . . at work in the fields." A popular song advised:

> *Just take your gun and go;*
> *For Ruth can drive the oxen, John,*
> *And I can use the hoe!*

For northerners, war meant fighting on distant battlefields. For southerners, the war raged close to home. With the menfolk away, women and children sought to preserve the homestead and the livestock by themselves. Youngsters might spend the night hiding in the canebrake with cows and oxen as foraging parties swept the area and the sky was lit by the flames of plantations and cotton warehouses that had been put to the torch.

The devastation was severe. By war's end much of the South was impoverished. Its one-crop economy was enfeebled. Its casualties had been high and its labor force was scattered. For many of those who came home there was nothing to build on. A new migration began, this time to the Texas cattle country.

By the end of the 1860's, half a million steers a year were being driven northward over several trails to the railhead at Abilene, where the stock could be shipped back to eastern markets.

A trail drive was one of the great adventures of the American past, although it probably did not seem very glamorous to the travel-stained cowboys who did the work. Each drive took several months. A herd properly broken to the routine of the trail could cover fifteen to twenty miles a day, grazing as it went. At dusk the cowboys bedded the cattle down for the night, and several of them rode in slow circles around the sleeping animals, singing or whistling to keep them calm. Off-duty cowboys slept on the ground with their clothes on and saddled horses nearby, ready for any emergency.

The trail boss rode on ahead, seeking a route that would assure water and grazing land. He was not always successful. One account of a crisis on the trail says: "The heat became almost unbearable to man and beast. . . . Over three days had now elapsed without water for the cattle, and they became feverish and ungovernable. The lead cattle turned back several times, wandering aimlessly in any direction. . . . The cattle gradually lost all semblance of a trail herd . . . milling and lowing in their fever and thirst. We threw our ropes in their faces, and when that failed we resorted to shooting . . . so close to the leaders' faces as to singe their hair, yet . . . they passed wholly out of control . . . deliberately walked against our horses, and then for the first time a fact dawned on us that chilled the marrow in our bones— *the herd was going blind.*"

Even when the weather behaved, danger threatened at all times. Indian attack was frequent. Rustlers' raids depleted the herds. Cattle were lost in quicksand and in the crossings of flooded rivers. And if the cattle were spooked—by lightning, the scent of a wild animal, or even a loud noise— there was the heart-stopping danger of a stampede. A sleeping herd would

The wild West deserved its reputation.
A man had to be tough to survive the rigors of the mining camp
or the cattle trail, with gunplay
a frequent adjunct of both. Very few were able to hang
onto their money. When the cowboys reached
Abilene, or the miners cashed in their gold, a night of
gambling and drinking would clean out
most; the others usually lost next time around.

*Plagued by the torturous terrain,
by weather, disease,
primitive facilities, hunger, and Indians—still
the people flocked to make the journey
west. With incredible
fortitude they came on, with little more
than their wits to help them
overcome the next seemingly insurmountable obstacle.
As the going became more difficult,
treasured possessions
were left by the wayside and reserves of courage
summoned to get them through.*

scramble to its feet and bolt, a mindless juggernaut overrunning anything that stood in its path, sometimes suicidally piling itself up in an arroyo. Riding at high speed, the cowboys tried to turn the herd back on itself, to break its momentum and reduce it to a milling, leaderless mob. If they were successful, the damage might be confined to a few dead and crippled animals. If not, the herd might have to run itself out and several days would have to be spent rounding it up.

But if there were times when he lived three days in the saddle without sleep, the cowboy could also remember the simple pleasures of yarning and singing around a fire under a velvet heaven full of stars, or the times when buffalo veal, or wild turkey eggs, or doughnuts varied the monotony of the trail diet. And beckoning at the end of every drive was Abilene. It was a cow town, to be sure, but it offered gambling and drinking and, for the man with money left over, fancy, red-topped boots, gaudy shirts, kerchiefs, and handsome silver trappings for bridle and saddle.

The cattle kingdom of the great West ranged from the Canadian border

to Mexico. Here the magnificent herds roamed free, taking grass where they found it. They grazed on public land and Indian territory alike, for few cattlemen could afford to own acreage vast enough to support their herds. But as the railroads pushed across the continent and the stream of homesteaders—encouraged by the Homestead Act of 1862—spread into state after state, conflicts arose. And since no satisfactory solution seemed possible, conflict erupted into war.

Cattlemen were enraged at the amount of grazing land being taken up by homesteaders' farms. Farmers were furious at the trampling of their crops by wandering herds. The invention of barbed wire was a huge assist to the farmer, but the barbs ripped enough cattle hides to lower the price the rancher received from the tanner and thereby kept the feud alive.

The cattleman also looked upon the sheepherder as an enemy. The flocks cropped the grass so close that there was little or nothing left for the herds. Since both were on Government land, however, neither had any call on the law. They fought as circumstances dictated and as the occasion afforded.

The Rocky Mountains
appeared to be impassable,
but a few had
crossed them and knew they
were not. These scouts
and guides, who knew what to
expect, led the settlers
across. The last day on the
plains meant a chance
for a final fortification
of body and spirit
before the ultimate push.

The sheepherder's life was even more lonely than the cowboy's. From June to September, while he pastured his several thousand sheep in the mountains, his bedroll was the only home he knew. The one or two visits of the supply wagon might be his only encounter with another human being—unless he ran afoul of cowboys. He worked for from $30 to $50 a month and keep.

In spite of hostile ranchers and warring Indians, the wagon trains came on. Most came because a neighbor, a son, or a brother had written home, urging others to join him. Nobody really believed that the cornstalks were tall enough to serve as telegraph poles, as the settlers loved to say, but the note of optimism from the West was enthusiastic and believable enough to draw the easterners on.

Fifteen years after Custer died at Little Big Horn, the Dakota prairies were yielding enormous quantities of wheat and beef. In the forty years after Lincoln became President, more than 400,000,000 acres, much of it beyond the Mississippi, were added to America's farmland. The United States became the greatest source of cheap food in the whole Atlantic world. To the list of heroic American characters—the hunter, the wilderness pioneer, the mountain man, the lone prospector—could now be added the prairie farmer. Men and women found nature both their adversary and their comfort on the prairie. Although many were broken by it, others bent it to their needs.

One of the richest prizes still sought by land-hungry whites was the Indian Territory, soon to be Oklahoma. Bowing to long pent-up pressure, the Government threw open the "Oklahoma District" on April 22, 1889. Twenty thousand boomers waited behind lines of soldiers until the trumpet blew at high noon. In a whirl of dust the stampeding men and women rushed in to stake out their claims before sundown.

More Indian tracts were turned over to whites in the following years. On September 16, 1893, the Cherokee Strip was opened. This time 100,000 awaited the signal to acquire a piece of the public domain. On horseback, in wagons, in anything on wheels, even on foot, the mass of people surged forward, seeing through the dust the land of their heart's desire. One woman, on a fiery little black pony, was said to have covered seven miles in seventeen minutes to reach a chosen homesite.

In the Northwest, too, Indians were shunted aside to make room for the white man's homestead, sheep and cattle ranches, and huge wheat farms.

Down into the Twentieth Century, Indian lands continued to be opened to homesteaders.

In the West, bonanza farms were organized along the lines of the large, new, industrial enterprises of the East. A wheat farm covering more than 10,000 acres was cut up into 2,000-acre divisions of self-contained units, with their own farm buildings, stables, and blacksmith shops. Most of the labor was supplied by migrants who followed the harvest from Kansas to Canada. Many were unemployed lumberjacks, who found that the pitchfork blistered even their already calloused hands. Harvest crews worked a thirteen-hour day on these oceans of grain and earned up to $12 a week per man, plus food and a place to sleep in the haymow.

In the South, agriculture was demoralized for some time after the Civil War. Most of the tools and livestock were gone. Drought and crop failures completed the ruin. A farmer was lucky to have a mule to draw his plow. Often enough men and women hitched themselves to the plow.

Negro slaves were now free, but most became tenant farmers and share-croppers whose lot was little improved over prewar days. For a week's work a farmhand got fifteen cents' worth of corn meal, thirty cents' worth of "fat-back," sixty cents in trade at the store, and twenty cents in cash. In addition to this $1.25, he got the yield from a two-acre truck patch he was allowed to work Saturday afternoons and evenings.

Cash was hard to come by, but the owner of the crossroads store willingly gave goods on credit to anyone who had prospects of reaping a crop. The store was a market where one could buy or sell. When a farmer sold, instead of taking cash for his cotton he had the sum entered in the big leather-bound ledger and charged his purchases against it. More often he bought first and brought the cotton later to settle his debts. This payment was regularly celebrated in the fall around the store's whiskey barrel. (Some of the raw liquor was taken home in a little brown jug for "the ole woman.") Tradition-ally, the mules knew their way home, so the farmer had no need to remain sober on this great day.

After the Civil War, whites as well as colored were in desperate need of all kinds of goods. In the North, manufacturers needed markets. New rail-roads needed freight, and encouraged the building of warehouses and retail outlets. Enterprising ex-soldiers came back to start in business for them-selves. Peddlers decided to sell merchandise from shelves, instead of carrying it around in a pack. Country stores mushroomed everywhere.

The Yankee peddler (and the Jewish peddler who followed him) had long

The Indians, constantly resentful

of the invasion of their land, attacked the

wagon trains unmercifully. It was

a common practice for the livestock to be herded into a circle

formed by the wagons at night. This gave

protection from marauders or rustlers, and helped prevent

the loss of strays. There was also some

comfort in the neighborly proximity afforded by the circle.

been a welcome visitor in rural areas. When he came into a home, beds were pushed back and room was made for his pack near the hearth, and the family gathered 'round for the show. With a flourish, the peddler opened the striped cover of his pack to display his stock: colored dress goods first, then the sweet-smelling perfumes and sachets, leather goods, knives, and nutmegs.

Long before he opened a store, the peddler knew his customers well. He had a good idea of what they wanted and how much credit he could extend. As a peddler he had been the source of news and gossip of the countryside. As a storekeeper, his door became the bulletin board for official notices of the activities and events of the town.

Exciting things happened at the store or else were immediately reported there: shootings, cuttings, deaths, births, marital troubles, courtings. Spacious grounds surrounding the store offered an ideal spot for picnics. The porch was a stump for politicians haranguing red-necked, tobacco-chewing constituents. The politician's words were more readily listened to when bourbon

The transcontinental railroad hastened the exchange of goods between East and West. Eastern manufacturers shipped their products to the frontier towns, which sent back cattle, sheep, and bait for the train robber— gold. Weather was a possible adversary, and many a train was waylaid by snow.

from the storehouse barrel was passed around freely. The space above the store was a temporary church or hall for lodge meetings.

Church members might grumble about that whiskey barrel, with its tin dipper, but male customers found it one of the store's major attractions. Next in popularity came the lunch counter, where the big blade of the cheese cutter sliced off "a nickel's worth" to go with a handful of crackers.

On Saturday a man, if he were fed up with the regular fare at home, could indulge in a store dinner of tempting foods from faraway places, such as canned sardines, salmon, sausages, and oysters. Those sardines, shiny with cottonseed oil and highly seasoned, accompanied by crackers, were the staple of every southern store. The real treat was a bowl full of canned, cove oysters, liberally doused with pepper sauce and eaten with crackers.

The everyday smell of the country store varied little, regardless of geography. It was a mellow blend of groceries and harness, horse collars and saddles, tobacco and whiskey, aging cheese, cabbage and onions, salt fish, turpentine and kerosene, and the mice that eluded the store's cat—all that plus the polish on the new shoes in the drawer.

Just as the odors were mixed, so was the stock. Everything was either under, behind, or over something else. Barrels on their racks were easiest to locate, so it was not difficult to find either whiskey or molasses. Also on racks were bags of flour, corn meal, and salt, as well as feed. Overhead hung red cedar buckets for hauling water. Elsewhere were plows, guns, axes, sledge hammers, and rope.

The storekeeper understood public relations long before it became a profession. His stove occupied the center of the store. Never was he known to object to the tobacco juice his customers aimed in its direction. Nor did he complain about the checker players and whittlers who rarely left their places around the stove where they sat on nail kegs, benches, or pine boxes. He was always ready to prescribe for a customer who might be suffering from rural ailments. He had a good stock of fancy patent medicines, as well as castor oil and Epsom salts. For youngsters he had peppermint sticks and licorice.

A partition faced with rows of locked boxes and a stamp window marked the post office. Its sacred precincts were off limits to the public. The storekeeper/postmaster, however, was always available to his customers and ready to help them with their correspondence. He wrote as well as read the farmer's letters for him. His patience was taxed only when a customer asked him to advance funds for a money order to be sent to Sears & Roebuck to buy goods available in his own store.

Mail-order houses caused a revolution in rural life. Country stores bitterly resented their competition and did what they could to destroy it. Catalogs were angrily burned by storekeepers. But it was a losing battle. Low prices and the alluring variety pictured in the "wish books" steadily diverted business to the distant company. Catalogs reflected the changing character of farm life. Wood stoves were supplanted by kerosene stoves, the "old oaken bucket" at the well by the kitchen pump, primitive lamps by bulbous, ornamented varieties.

In New England, not even the mail-order houses did good business, however. Farmers there had continued to drift away from the land, to go west, or to nearby cities. The local complaint was that "farming does not pay." The countryside looked neglected, with fences sagging, buildings in disrepair, and highways lined with brush. Abandoned farms were up for sale. An advertisement in the 1890's described a typical one:

*Bonanza farms in the West were organized
along the lines of the large, new industrial developments in the
East. A wheat farm of ten thousand acres was divided
into self-contained units of two thousand acres, each with its
own buildings. Most of the workers
were migrants who followed the harvest from Kansas to
Canada. During the harvest season, these men worked a thirteen-hour
day for room, board, and about $12 a week.*

"Farm of sixty acres; mowing, eight; pasture, eighteen; woodland, thirty-four; suitable for cultivation, twelve. Almost all the grass can be cut with a machine. One-story house, five rooms, in need of some repair. Small barn, in good repair. Good well at house, and running water back of barn. Twenty apple and twelve other fruit trees. Railroad station, Leverett, six miles; post office, Shutesbury, one mile. Price, $400; cash at sale $100; interest on balance, four percent."

While the discouraged farmers moved away, the more persistent found that new uses for old soils could eventually be made profitable. The East could not compete with the West in raising wheat and corn. Corn cost twice as much in New England as it did in the Middle West. On the prairie, stoneless fields could be worked by reapers and gang plows that would be useless on New England's small, stone-walled plots.

The future of New England agriculture had been foretold even before the Civil War by William Buckminster. Don't worry about the cheap midwestern grain, he told farmers. Supply what cannot be brought easily from a distance. Fresh meats, hay, dairy products, vegetables—these are the things New England should produce. "The times are changed," Buckminster said, "and we must change with them."

Farmers who took his advice did well. Specialization paid. And although countrymen often scoffed at "book farming," state agricultural colleges were able to improve strains of poultry and cattle. Truck crops—cabbage, lettuce, potatoes, cucumbers, celery, onions—found good, steady markets.

Tobacco proved to be a bonanza crop. It had been popular since the early days. The Puritans smoked it in pipes or drank the juice added to punch. Despite early laws against it, it was recognized as a habit hard to break and for generations tobacco culture throve. By the early Nineteenth Century factories in New England were producing thousands of handmade cigars daily. Not long after, the whole lower valley of the Connecticut was planted to tobacco.

Orchards brought in welcome cash, although a large portion of the apple crop, turned into applejack, was consumed locally. Even modest-sized orchards produced over five hundred barrels of cider. With a cider press and distillery, weary tillers of the soil found a profitable new occupation.

Abandoned farms were not always sold to other farmers. Businessmen, lawyers, doctors, and teachers bought them for country homes where they could spend vacations and week ends away from the tensions of city life. Artists' colonies grew up in secluded spots favored by enchanting views. Many a farmer was able to hold on to the family homestead by taking in summer boarders.

In many respects country life had remained unchanged over the years. The farmer wore boots, when he was not barefoot or all dressed up for church, because most of the time he walked on damp, spongy topsoil. A footscraper at the door removed the mud from his boots.

The outdoor privy had not yet given way to an indoor water closet. During the night the chamber pot saved a trip to the outhouse. The Saturday night bath was a ritual. The portable tub was set before the fireplace, partly filled with cold water, and only enough hot water was added from the kettle to take off the chill.

Adjoining the kitchen was the spring room. Water from the spring was piped to a barrel that fed a sink whose drain took care of the overflow. This offered running water to a farm kitchen, except in drought when springs could run dry. The spring itself, some distance from the house, was covered

Work may have seemed
almost endless, but the early
country-dwellers could
sustain themselves
with the beauty of the land
they lived in:
*the frosty marvel of an unravaged
Vermont forest at
maple-sugaring time, or the
view—even from a poor cottage—
of Lookout Mountain.*

AMERICAN FOREST SCENE.
MAPLE SUGARING.

73

Many labor-saving inventions were produced to lighten the
burdens of the farmer, but his dress, surroundings, and way of life actually changed
very little with the passage of time, or from place to place.

by a springhouse, shaded by a large tree. It was always cool there; even on a hot summer day the dipper was ready to provide a refreshing drink.

The root cellar, partly underground, contained potatoes, carrots, cabbage, and turnips gathered before the frost. Piled in bins, the root vegetables were well protected, and promised ample food for the table until late spring, when dandelion greens and mushrooms came along to add variety. Apples laid out on straw perfumed the cellar. On the shelves stood jars of preserved vegetables and fruits, jellies, jams, and apple butter.

Cider vinegar was used to transform cucumbers into tantalizing pickles. It also pickled pigs' sides, and was mixed with molasses for Saturday night's baked beans.

When cold weather arrived for certain, the butchering of hogs began. Knife and ax were sharpened on a grindstone and soon the smokehouse was hung with hams and sausages curing in a pungent blend of sugar, salt, spices, and smoldering hickory.

Weather determined many of the farm's activities. The farmer kept his eye on the weathervane, he scanned the cloud formations, and he watched the phases of the moon. From these observations he determined the best time to saw timber, make sauerkraut, gather apples, shear sheep, or harvest grain. He also developed a number of persuasive maxims concerning weather behavior that were not very good meteorology, but turned out right just often enough to become an imperishable part of American folklore:

If it rains before seven,
It will be clear before eleven.

When the dew is on the grass,
Rain will never come to pass.

Schooling was a different matter. The only auspicious time for education was when the children could be spared from the farm. Usually this meant a few months in the winter and a few weeks in the summer. But for the most part, despite the respect in which education was held, youngsters could think of far more interesting things to do in their spare time. A boy could hunt rabbits or go fishing in the brook, while his dog kept him company. But the law insisted on his learning to read, write, and do sums.

The one-room school was not always "the little red." Sometimes it was white, but little it was, and it had a bell in the cupola to summon unwilling scholars to its drab interior. The pupils, from five to twenty years old, fidgeted on the hard benches, hoping not to attract the attention of a teacher who was ever ready to wield a birch rod.

The teacher's life was not an enviable one. He—or she—boarded at a nearby farmhouse and began the school day early, building a fire in the stove, sweeping the cold, musty room, and cleaning the blackboard, as well as educating the children. For all this the community paid $20 to $30 a month.

The children arrived early, too, quite possibly after a long walk through the dust of summer's heat or the cold of a bleak winter. Recess, mid-morning or mid-afternoon, made the tedious hours in between seem less unbearable. The girls played tag or jumped rope, the boys played marbles or catch.

Only at Christmastime did many of the children look forward to the trip to school. The family dressed in its finest, piled into "the one-horse open sleigh," and was off to the sound of jingling bells. That night, school did not look like school at all. Parents and children crowded inside, where there was a gaudy Christmas tree in the corner and bright-colored paper chains and strings of popcorn hanging from anything offering anchor. Everyone sang Christmas songs to the accompaniment of the little organ.

The big event of the evening came when Santa Claus appeared to pass around his gifts of oranges and striped candy canes. Throughout the performance of the long-rehearsed pageant on the tiny makeshift stage, all ears had been cocked for the sleigh bells that announced his arrival.

The conscientious farmer had little time for recreation, but the occasions he did observe were likely to be major events for the whole family. At Thanksgiving, for example, normal activity in the farmhouse stopped to allow for the preparation of an elaborate feast and getting ready to entertain the many relatives who would arrive by railroad.

Everyone trooped off to the county fair that came in September. This was a three-day affair and, if possible, they went every day. Those who lived far away came in big lumber wagons, prepared for camping. The farm's prize produce was on exhibit and there was stiff rivalry for the blue ribbons.

The animals, all spruced up for show in the tents, seemed comically out of place to the children. Standing quietly amid the human excitement, they looked wooden, like toy animals, although at home each one revealed a distinct personality. The children remembered when the newborn lamb, its silky coat still wet, had been brought to the kitchen and kept warm in back of the stove. They had watched it grow day by day and knew all its tempers. At the fair it seemed a stranger.

On display nearby was the New England-bred Morgan horse. Called "the poor man's horse," it was equally adept at drawing plow, buggy, or sled. Vermont farmers considered themselves experts at judging its qualities. At another booth, a grandmother hovered near her patchwork quilt and carefully noted the tricky patterns of others that might be judged more attractive. Father was the only member of the family interested in the plows and new-fangled machines being shown in a far corner of the field. From there he soon moved off surreptitiously to the peep show for his annual fling at vice.

Greed was the special indulgence of the youngsters. It got full play at the fair. They splurged on candy and other enticements until their precious coins

The Yankee peddler was
always a welcome visitor in any rural
area. He was a source
of countryside news and gossip, and
a showman as well. It was with
true dramatic flair that he displayed his
wares to the assembled family.

A unique center for social activity
was the general store. Crammed with an unimaginable
variety of merchandise, it also served
as the focal point of the widespread community.

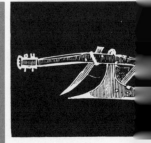

were gone, then stood drooling while judges sampled mince pies and layer cakes that looked and smelled agonizingly tempting.

On the midway, leather-lunged hawkers called strollers to games of chance —lotteries, a shell game ("now you see it, now you don't")—until the sheriff came along. Minstrels and a merry-go-round added their music to the shouts and squeals coming from the contest to catch the greased pig.

The biggest thrill of the fair was the spectacular balloon act that marked the end of the day. A man wearing a parachute and balanced precariously on a trapeze was hauled aloft by the great canvas balloon. When he was only a waving speck in the sky, he made his death-defying jump to earth. The collapsed balloon drifted to a nearby hilltop—exhausted like most of the spectators, who were now ready for home and bed.

County fairs came in the fall. In June there might be a country auction— perhaps the sale of an entire farm—to provide another chance to meet, compete, and get away from the farm. The lunch served on the lawn by ladies of the church made a picnic of it. Some folks came just for the show and sociability. Some came to buy things they really needed at bargain prices. Others bought what they scarcely wanted only to outbid someone else. But the auctioneer got his commission on every item. He was an old hand at keeping the customers entertained with his jokes.

Small items were jumbled together as "lots" in baskets or barrels. The farmer's order had been to sell the old place "lock, stock, and barrel." Although the owners hovered in the background through most of the sale, suffering in silence, they added their sales talk at the end, when the farm itself was up for bidding. Then the owner showed samples of corn and wheat to prove the land's fertility and his wife vouched for the dependable supply of water in the well.

Throughout the orderly seasons
of childhood, boys and girls awaited the
celebration of Christmas, and
the excitement it brought to their quiet country homes.
Presents might not be extravagant, but anticipation
of the event was itself a reward.

Sometimes they themselves bid on a favorite animal or a piece of furniture that at the last moment they could not bear to part with. Later, antique dealers would show interest in the drop-leaf table, the corner cupboard, the rope bed, and the rocker that grandfather had made—things that had always been taken for granted.

The farm itself would go to a young farmer and his bride who were ready to start a new life in an old setting. The date grandfather had carved in the adzed surface of the heavy oak beam in the attic remained to tell the new owners when he had constructed the house—although he had built it for his own descendants, never dreaming that his handiwork one day would be sold to strangers.

The aging eastern farmer sold his place at auction because his bones were aching and he was not "enjoying his pie" anymore. He felt he could no longer maintain the farm without his children there to help. He was finally ready to accept their invitation to join them in the West.

Instead of being surrounded by the deserted farms he had become accustomed to at home, he found himself amid vast fields of corn and waving

*Education was a luxury
for children who could be spared
from the farm. For the students
it was at best an uncomfortable business, always
subject to the danger of incurring the
underpaid teacher's wrath.*

grain. The steampower that ran the train which brought him and his wife to Illinois also ran the machines the young folks were using to help with the farm work.

The young western farmer's house was small—two rooms downstairs and two under the gabled roof. The stairway was on the outside, so it was decided that the old folks should sleep downstairs. It was not the house itself, but the furnishings that impressed the parents. Obviously, their son had prospered. He had a coal stove in the kitchen and his wife did her sewing and washing with the aid of machines. Their lamps burned coal-oil (kerosene) and threw a sharp glare. There was a special, zinc-lined wooden tub for the Saturday-night bath.

The furniture was not homemade, either; it came from a factory with modern production methods. The son had also developed modern ideas. He was careful how he stored the barnyard manure for fertilizer. "Mosquito bar" screens at the windows kept out the flies. He said it was important to put the privy far from the spring and on a slope that slanted away from it. He told the old man about a friend who had gone to college. (Land-grant colleges were being established all through the West.) It was this friend who had aroused his interest in hygiene and new farming methods, recommending that he subscribe to an agricultural journal.

The old man questioned his grandchildren about their schooling. (New Englanders prided themselves on their concern for education.) First he wanted to know if theirs was a "loud school"—did the pupils study their lessons in the classroom by reading *aloud* to themselves? It pleased him to hear that the educators' old stand-bys were still used—McGuffey's readers, Ray's arithmetic, and Webster's blue-back speller.

A girl was admired if she were smart in school, a boy was ridiculed. Naturally, the girl did better. She would be missed by her teacher when she left; a good student was about the only genuine recompense a teacher had.

Teaching both summer and winter sessions might bring in $100 for the year, less than a farm laborer earned. Many a male teacher turned laborer between sessions. Hard physical work augmented income; it also kept him in trim for maintaining discipline.

Older members of the family were invited to compete in the Friday afternoon spelling bees and ciphering contests. They also used the schoolhouse and grounds for their box suppers, literary and scientific lectures, and as a meeting place for the various religious groups in the community.

At threshing time in July, a young man could combine work and pleasure if he belonged to a team of threshers. At every farm in the "ring"—on the circuit—the women-folk outdid themselves to make a royal feast for the threshermen, and to smile their prettiest smiles while they served them at the long tables.

Platters of crisp, golden, fried chicken, and more platters of juicy pink ham were accompanied by vegetables and potatoes (mashed or creamed) with lots of gravy. And homemade bread kept coming with fresh butter and all kinds of jellies and preserves. The milk was good and cold. Hot coffee arrived with apple pies and chocolate cakes. Then, after the feasting was over, the women came out in new aprons and sunbonnets to watch the threshers work their wonderful machines. This went on, at farm after farm, for days. For many young men, tilling the soil in the Midwest was a very satisfying way of life.

The three-day county fair
that came in September was a must for the
whole family. There
were contests for everyone. Grandmother could
enter her best patchwork, father
his prize bull, mother a sample of her
apple pie, and the
children their pen of lambs. The midway offered
entertainment for all, with
a spectacular balloon act as a finale.

It was the old folks who now began to fix their eyes on the Far West's bright horizon. Much was being said of the West Coast's golden sunshine and year-around warmth. It was 1875 when young Luther Burbank went to California from New England and discovered for himself the wonders of Sonoma Valley, north of San Francisco. After a few days he wrote: "I firmly believe . . . that it is the chosen spot of all this earth as far as nature is concerned . . . I have almost to cry for joy when I look upon the lovely valley from the hillside." In time, this and many other valleys were to be made even lovelier by his experiments that resulted in new varieties of fruits, berries, vegetables, and flowers.

Even before California joined the United States, oranges were a California specialty. By the turn of the century, they were a major factor in the economy. To market the state's crop (and bring in new settlers) an advertising campaign in the Middle West, in 1907, blazed the slogan, "Oranges for Health—California for Wealth." Iowa, where the campaign was concentrated, waited excitedly for the first fruit train to arrive. Newspapers carried cartoons of a blond-haired beauty feeding oranges to a sickly youngster labeled "Iowa." Orange sales boomed and Iowans moved to California by the thousands.

They all looked forward to a life free from worry about being snowbound

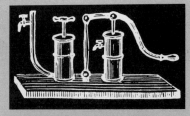

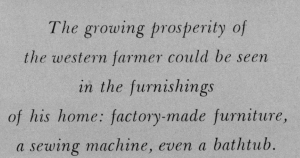

The growing prosperity of
the western farmer could be seen
in the furnishings
of his home: factory-made furniture,
a sewing machine, even a bathtub.

or getting stuck in the mud of unimproved country roads. For although the Midwest produced flourishing crops, it had its problems. In addition to capricious weather, prices were low, mortgages were burdensome, and the farmer felt he was being ignored by the politician. To add insult to injury, the city folk laughed at him, calling him "rube" and "hayseed." His answer was to join the Granger movement, the first organized attempt to seek legislation beneficial to the farmer. Under the goad of slogans urging them to "raise less corn and more hell," farmers flocked to the Grange until the membership totaled a million and a half. Local Granges met once a month to discuss farm problems, to gossip, and to sing. Children from isolated farms enjoyed playing with others of their age. On occasion all worked together to raise money and supplies for farmers in areas where disaster had struck. Eventually, Grangers were to be a powerful factor in the Democratic party and in securing the nomination of William Jennings Bryan for the presidency.

Despite the Grange's assurance of his importance, the farmer faced conditions on his farm that often were too discouraging to warrant continuing the struggle. He weighed the alternatives. Should he look for better farmland? Or should he go to a nearby factory or mill town to get a job and live in a boarding house?

*Unable to compete with the West in the grain
market, New Englanders turned to specialization. Northeastern agriculture
came to mean fresh poultry, dairy products, fruits and
vegetables—items that could not easily be shipped long distances.*

FAIR

KENTON, IA.
SEPT. 10·13, '89

A PLACE TO STUDY AND LEARN

The Progress of Invention and the Development of Mechanical Ingenuity.

MULTIPLIED ATTRACTIONS!

Entertainment and Amusement on a Mammoth Scale.

The Managers have Information giving Assurance of the most

NOTEWORTHY & SUCCESSFUL

Fair Ever Held Upon Their Grounds.

ELECTRIFYING RACES
SPLENDID BAND MUSIC

Wearing a stylish mail-order suit, hat, and shoes, however, sometimes gave him bigger ideas. Not only the citified clothes, but descriptions of city life that he had been accumulating from his reading of newspapers and illustrated weeklies had opened new vistas. Now the whistle of a passing train sounded more insistent. The lure was great enough to tempt large numbers of farm boys to the city. The oldsters remaining on the land tried to stem the flow:

Come, boys, I have something to tell you,
  Come near, I will whisper it low;
You are thinking of leaving the homestead,
  Don't be in a hurry to go.
The city has many attractions,
  But think of the vices and sins,
When once in the vortex of fashion
  How soon the course downward begins.
Stay on the farm, stay on the farm,
  Though profits come in rather slow.
Stay on the farm, stay on the farm;
  Don't be in a hurry to go.

Many a young man who was afraid to risk the wicked city decided to move to a neighboring town. Towns were less frightening. Not every one you met there was a stranger, and the place held few surprises: the stores bordering a block-long pavement, with hitching rails; storekeepers never too busy to pass the time of day; the park with its grass and shade trees, its bandstand and benches—all this was comfortable and familiar.

To an ambitious young man, the town offered the chance to become a trained mechanic, perhaps even a doctor or lawyer. He could earn enough money to go to college, and then return to serve an apprenticeship in the office of a professional man. Later, he would inherit his mentor's practice. Some day a successful young man who had left the farm might own one of those white houses on a tree-shaded street. The smooth lawn would be edged with a white picket fence—and his shingle would hang at the door. For such as this, many a boy would leave the open country of his youth to establish his own roots in the close-knit community that was the town.

The virtues of farm life as extolled by
the Grange were many, but so were the economic problems
that beset the farmer. In spite of the beauty
of the land that was his heritage, the young man from the country
was increasingly drawn to the attractions of urban life.

The *VIL*

LAGE

*The New England farmer going to town usually had one road
to travel. Usually, it wound through small green hills, crossed a
rocky stream on the rattling planks of a covered bridge, . . .*

. . . and led in due course to the Common.
Here milch cows browsed on the grass, it was cool in the shade of ancient
elms, and here the life of the town was centered. A serene white church or
meetinghouse stood at one end of the green, the residence of the town's
most important man was often at the other. On either side might be the
humbler homes of lesser citizens, the store, the smithy, and the tavern. Farther
on, beside a stream where the water ran swiftly, was the gristmill. Depending
on the year, the region, and the town's metabolism, there might also be a
cabinet maker, a silversmith, a weaver, a printer.

From the nucleus the town grew outward in a random pattern dictated by

the fertility of the soil, the availability of water, and a man's stomach for clearing a homesite out of the encroaching forest. Beyond this, the land reached back, over the bridge and through the hills, to the scattered rural farms. All else was wilderness.

This was the essential town. Its like could be found in the late Eighteenth Century throughout the recently united states. There were local variations, of course. Taste, custom, and climate accentuated differences; New Hampshire would never be mistaken for South Carolina. Yet everywhere the structure of the town was recognizable. The church bell pealed over the land, summoning the congregation to prayer. The general store traded briskly in the luxuries and necessities of the day. The smith's bellows blew the forge hot and sparks flew as wheel rims, hinges, and gun barrels were beaten into shape on the anvil. The mossy waterwheel turned leisurely at the mill, the wooden gears creaked, and the rugged millstones reduced the farmer's grain to flour. On their rounds through the village, people exchanged news

and gossip. In the tavern, the lounger, the traveler, the countryman homeward-bound stopped for a noggin of rum or a tankard of ale.

It was a placid life, still somewhat colonial, but quickening to the demands of new conditions and new ideas. The spring of the Nineteenth Century was a season of great growth. The cities reached outward to the towns, seeking markets for their goods, manpower for their factories, and routes to other cities. The towns burgeoned and drew closer to the country.

Not all of them, to be sure, but many. Some towns grew through accidents of geography. Valley towns, lying athwart broad natural highways, flourished. So did towns offering safe harbor from the sea and those which were fortunately perched as way stations or terminals for stagecoaches, riverboats, or canal barges. Some towns grew because they met the needs of cattlemen driving stock to the railhead.

The railroads themselves planted towns at junction points and depots. You could always recognize a railroad town. It was laid out in a gridiron pattern. The North-South streets were given the names of trees, the cross streets were numbered. Some were built with a square at the center and stores on all four sides. In the square was a bandstand. Great sums were spent to lure settlers to these towns. Free building sites were offered to storekeepers and newspaper editors, responsible and persuasive types who could be depended on to attract others.

Some towns assured their prominence by managing to be named the county seat. Others boomed when they were found to be sitting on silver, copper, coal, and oil.

In Montana and other western territories, little frontier towns prospered by relieving cowboys of their hard-earned cash. The trail hands were willing. As they drove their herds over the weary miles, they hankered for the day they would ford the Yellowstone River and ride into Frenchman's Ford or any one of a hundred towns like it.

They visited the barber for a shave ("two bits"). They bought fancy shirts and toured the saloons and gambling resorts, ready to pick a fight just for excitement. More than half of the houses were canvas. Great numbers of buffalo hides were drying in the sun for shipment. Ox-train drivers swaggered down the street, mingling with buffalo hunters, scouts, and Indians and their squaws wrapped in gaudy blankets and red calico. It wasn't much but it was a town, you bet.

Sometimes a community grew without lifting a finger. Lord's Bridge, Connecticut, for one. Things had remained pretty much the same for at least three generations when one day an outsider, a "hustler" seeking a mill site, stopped for a while on the bridge and looked the place over. The Shetucket River was rushing along noisily beneath him, the surrounding countryside was attractive.

He bought three hundred acres and built a cotton mill five stories high and a thousand feet long. Within five years there were a hundred homes, a church, a school, and stores. People flocked in from as far away as Canada to work in what was now the country's biggest mill.

Only the remotest corners of

the land were now beyond the reach of the rivers, the

railroads, and the highways. Regions

differed, but the people were united as Americans.

In time, towns become known for a specialty. Hitchcock chairs made in Barkhamstead, Connecticut, or fine hats made in Danbury brought fame and profit to their communities. Mass production enabled small towns to turn out hundreds of thousands of mousetraps, thousands of candlesticks, and hundreds of axes a day for shipment to Central and South America, as well as to country stores throughout the United States. The manufacture of clocks, brass, and firearms gave employment to thousands.

By mid-century, towns both north and south began to acquire an appearance and character that would be recognizable today. They were becoming the old-fashioned towns of our grandparents' childhood. At their heart—the main street—these towns had two rows of one-story wooden buildings. The occasional brick structure of two or three stories stood out ostentatiously. It provided offices for the lawyer or doctor, and the large hall on the second floor was an "Opera House" or the lodge of a fraternal order, perhaps the Masons. The Opera House was rarely for opera, but the name lent respectability—although show people themselves were still somewhat suspect. Along Main Street the sidewalks meandered up and down steps. Wooden platforms, built to the height of a wagon bed to make unloading easy, ran from the sidewalk's edge to a store's front door.

Some of the white clapboard homes were two stories high. Unlike the rough log cabins of the frontier, they were made of smooth lumber from the sawmill. More pretentious houses were plastered or built of homemade brick. Their

Politics and judicial
procedure were still the province of the
male, and he made spirited use of
them. A good trial at the
courthouse or a local election
drew large crowds of
spectators and participants. They managed
to fortify their civic concern
with frequent trips to the whiskey keg.

A bountiful table was the symbol
of independence. The family might be cut off by bad weather,
but as long as there was wood for
the fire and a good supply of preserved foods, it was safe.

shingled roofs might be topped with as many as five chimneys. In time, in the settled, more comfortable, and increasingly successful towns, architecture became more than a matter of shelter, available materials, and economic status. It became an expression of taste. Greek Revival was the style. Towns took Greek names—Sparta, Athens—and stolid carpenters were given illustrated building manuals showing handsome structures with Greek columns that they were expected to copy as best they could.

Ionic or clapboard, the homes were hard to heat. Downstairs a family depended on stoves or the open hearth. Upstairs, the hot metal stovepipes fought the chill. Bedwarmers, filled with hot coals, helped combat the clammy cold of bedding and sleepers used feather quilts above and below.

In the bedrooms, a "commode" closeted the chamber pot that served in the absence of indoor plumbing. Water for washing stood in a pitcher on the commode and came from the rain barrel under the eave spout.

Pine knots, grease lamps, and candles were on the way out. The principal source of light was the oil lamp, with wick, glass chimney, and shade. Its soft glow made the polished oak floors and paneled doors glisten in the night and the shadowed staircase became a thing of beauty.

Small-towners were early risers, like farmers. Breakfast was still a meal. The family gathered around the big table in the dining room to eat a bowl of oatmeal or corn-meal mush, some meat or sausages, and boiled eggs with thick slices of homemade bread well-buttered. (In the South, hotbreads were the rule: muffins, beaten biscuit, rolls.) Mother was up early to prepare the food, but she waited for the family to begin eating before she started the griddle-cakes sizzling. These were a special treat. Plenty of coffee and tea for adults; for children, milk that came to the table in a pitcher.

This was supposed to satisfy you until midday dinner when all the family, including father home from work, came to the dining table again. Dinner began with soup. Then the roast was presented (beef, ham, or mutton) for father to carve, and chicken, duck, turkey, or wild game, as well. The vegetables were fresh from a nearby farm.

Mother, erect at her end of the table, served dessert: pudding or pie, maybe both. She loved to watch her family dining well. It was her job and her pride to see that they were properly fed.

A bountiful table gave her and her family a sense of independence and self-sufficiency that made them relatively free of the outside world. They might be cut off by heavy snowstorms, but they could still remain comfortable with their oil lamps, a pile of wood to feed the stove, jars of preserves and pickled or smoked meat stored away in the cellar. Many families even had a cow in the barn.

The dining room was the center of the home mother created. In the middle of it stood the round table. It had extension leaves so that it could be enlarged for company. Between meals it was covered with a Turkey-red cloth, on which stood a well-filled fruit bowl. After supper the family sat around the table again, children to do homework, mother to do her mending. If there was time, father read aloud from the books the children received for Christmas: Cooper's *Leatherstocking Tales* or Irving's *Sketch Book* (the children knew Rip Van Winkle by heart).

In wealthier homes, a silver tea set stood on the top of an elaborate sideboard. In the two drawers were stored the silverware and table linen. It was no secret from the children that the double doors at the bottom of the sideboard hid the cookie tin. Doughnuts or sugar-frosted cookies with a raisin in the middle were always there in good supply.

Separating the kitchen, with its big iron stove and its cooking odors, from the dining room with its elegance, was a serving pantry. Along its wall were the cupboards for china and glasses. Below the cupboards ran a long counter where the food was lined up for presentation during the meal. Afterward the dishes were stacked here to be washed in the pantry sink.

Even in less pretentious homes meals were eaten leisurely. Work, too, was unhurried, leaving time for talk, the favorite recreation. Housecleaning and the family wash were, on occasion, allowed to wait while the latest word crossed and recrossed the back fences. No one was born, no one was married, nobody died without the back-yard gossips telling it all in detail.

The weekly schedule had a certain reassuring regularity. Clothes were washed on Monday with the aid of tub and washboard. Each housewife aimed to be first in getting the wash hung out on the line in the yard. Tuesday it was ironed with flatirons heated on the kitchen stove; starched ruffles took time and patience. Wednesday was for sewing and patching. Thursday was

After an uncomfortable day in a springless stagecoach
or wagon, the traveler paused for refreshment and rest at a roadside
tavern. The sympathetic host was ofttimes a former driver.

for incidentals like fancywork—crocheting or embroidery. Friday the house was cleaned. Carpets were swept with a broom, the housewife wearing a dust cap. Kitchen floors and the porches were scrubbed on hands and knees. The stoves were polished and everything was dusted, including the figurines on the shelves of the whatnot in the corner. Saturday was baking day: pies, cakes, cookies, and doughnuts were homemade. Ice cream, too, but a boy might be glad to turn the handle of the freezer for the privilege of licking the dasher. Sunday was for church and company.

Spring brought special chores. Spring cleaning was a major operation. The man's job was to remove the storm windows. A boy could swat at the carpets on the line with a carpet beater. With frost out of the ground, a small garden could be spaded for a row of sweet corn, of beans, and another of tomatoes, plus some radishes and lettuce.

Women broke off a few branches of forsythia to set in a sunny window and bring spring indoors. The wren house was cleaned and made ready for an early tenant. The first robin strutting on the lawn was welcomed as a sign that the long winter was over. The swing was painted and suspended from the hooks of the porch ceiling. Here, in the warm weather ahead, the lady of the house could rest from her duties. On a summer evening it was here that her daughter entertained a beau.

Being seen in public places was an incentive to "getting dressed up." The women who could afford it patronized the town's dressmakers and milliners instead of sewing for themselves. They wanted imported materials for their clothes, to be fastened with pretty buttons instead of hooks. And they wanted fine straw for their hats instead of rye straw. No calico sunbonnets, either. They carried parasols to protect their peaches-and-cream complexions.

Years before the Civil War, men in some western towns were influenced by the ads for stylish frock coats and fancy trousers. They bought vests, cravats, and handkerchiefs of imported silk. There were many "dandies" among them who insisted on a pastel broadcloth coat, adorned with gold-plated buttons, to be worn with tight-fitting pants. (An eastern dandy of an earlier day, ordering his tight trousers, warned his tailor, "If I can get into 'em, I won't pay for 'em.")

Even the children were dressed in imitation of adult fashion, instead of wearing clothes made over from the worn-out homespun garments of the grown-ups. It was an exciting experience for a country boy to be fitted out at the store for his school outfit. Hamlin Garland told of standing with his brother like "sturdy hitching posts" while "the storekeeper with heavy hands screwed cotton plush caps" on their heads. "The crowning joy of the day came with the buying [of] new boots," said Garland, who added regretfully, "If only father had not insisted on our taking those which were a size too large for us." Garland was especially pleased that, unlike other boys' boots, his did *not* have copper toes. He feasted his eyes on his purchase, red tops with a golden moon in the center.

Sophisticated townsfolk also began wearing underwear! Soldiers in the Civil War were surprised to be issued drawers. Some believed the prankster who said that they were part of a special dress uniform!

The life of the town was still dependent on the horse. Barns and carriage sheds were built close to the main house. Harness-makers and blacksmiths were in every community. Hitching racks and watering troughs were conveniently located. Cemeteries were placed near enough to town so that the horse-drawn hearse and funeral carriages did not have to be too long on the road.

The village blacksmith was an important personality. The old saying that your horse's feet were no better than your blacksmith indicated the high regard in which a good craftsman was held. The pungent smell of a horse's hoof being fitted was an odor that drifted out into the street. The solid clang of hammer on anvil was remembered long after it rang no more.

The livery stable, where horses and rigs were hired, smelled of liniment and leather, hay and manure. Its plank floor resounded to the pounding of hoofs after the horses came up the ramp through the large doors to return to their stalls. Near the front of the stable was a dingy office with a cot, some chairs, a pot-bellied stove, and a banged-up old desk. A lantern hung from the wall to light the way for night customers.

Large livery stables rented spring wagons to salesmen making the rounds of country stores. Fancy buggies were available for a suitor and his girl; fringed surreys served for double dates. A carryall, with steps in the rear leading up to the seats along the sides, took parents and children to picnics, visiting baseball teams to the town's diamond, or old folks bearing flowers to the cemetery on Memorial Day. The doctor kept his horse and carriage at the stable, the hotel its hack. Beside the door was a reminder to:

Whip Light,
Drive Slow.
Pay Cash
Before You Go.

Inland waterways were developed and sported craft of every known type, but the steamboat brought efficiency and luxury to transportation.

The town loafers found the stable a favorite meeting place. They snickered at those who referred to bulls as "gentleman cows" and stallions as "gentleman horses." The livery-stable crowd did not belong to refined society. Their dress was slovenly and their language direct and profane. But small boys were fascinated. They loved to curry horses and climb over buggies; stoically they mucked out the stalls. Sex was no mystery to a small boy who spent his time at the stable.

Town storekeepers were not yet tied to big city business which, in time, was to pressure them into selling packaged and branded wares. General stores still sold calico and coffee, butter, cheese, sugar, and flour in bulk. Inaccurate measuring of piece goods led to insistence that tacks be nailed to the counter to indicate thirty-six inches. "Come down to brass tacks" was the customer's demand for fair measure.

The merchandise in the general store was often strewn about topsy-turvy. Crackers in an open barrel were stale and fly-specked. The colors on yard goods often were not fast, although "oil-boiled" calico was reliable. The fit of clothing was hit or miss, and the durability of textiles doubtful.

But if quality and variety might be wanting, the business of buying and selling was usually informal and friendly. In a community of seven or eight hundred souls, everyone knew everyone else. By and large, everyone patronized the same stores, had the same opinions, and lived the same lives. Hamlin Garland remembered shopkeepers as friends, dispensing sugar and kerosene while attired in shirt sleeves, a long apron, and a derby. Store owners, he said, "were not only my neighbors, but members of the Board of Education."

Folks met at the general store, at the hardware store with its washtubs and clothes baskets, stepladders and garden tools, or at the meat market. First names came naturally and there was usually time to stop for a chat.

The breathless gossip of children concerned the gypsies who were supposed to be horse thieves. There was considerable excitement when they arrived in their colorful wagons to set up a temporary camp on the outskirts of town. Youngsters knew gypsies "stole horses and kidnapped children!" This did not stop a boy from spying on the exotic strangers. The gaudy dresses of the women, the flashing eyes of the men, even the strange smells of their outdoor cooking were too fascinating to be missed. Grown-ups might take the opportunity to have their fortunes told, but they were also careful to lock up their horses.

At the barber shop it was a man's world. Conversation was long and full of belly laughs. While a man waited for a shave and haircut, he could also read the shocking pink pages of the *Police Gazette*.

Being seen in public places was incentive to get dressed up. Women who could afford it patronized dressmakers and milliners; some purchased trinkets from the door-to-door salesman. Even the men were becoming stylish. They wore frock coats and elegantly-cut trousers. The children no longer were dressed in hand-me-downs, but as miniature adults.

*Nearby woods and streams
often lured townspeople out for an all-day
picnic. An elaborate feast set
under the trees was the primary diversion, but while their
elders rested and gossiped,
the children played games or searched for new
treasures for their collections, and
young couples momentarily escaped their chaperones.*

The barber shop was usually near the billiard parlor. A heavy cloud of cigar smoke was common to both, but the barber shop mixed the odor of cigars with the scent of bay rum and tonic. Fancy shaving mugs lined the wall; each regular customer had his own with his mark on it. Even the basins and water pitchers were lavishly decorated and mirrors added glitter. A polished brass spittoon stood beside each red velour barber chair. Before the average home could boast a bathroom, a man might pay the barber twenty-five cents for soap and towel and the privilege of using the shop's bathtub.

Towns offered a variety of recreation, some simple, some sophisticated, depending on the cultural inclinations of the inhabitants. Out west, young and old gathered at the courthouse whenever it was known that a famous circuit lawyer would be arguing a case. A visitor to a "straggling western village" on the Missouri frontier in 1848 wrote: "The session of Court attracted a considerable number of country people to the town, and these were principally collected about a miserable, naked-looking edifice made of mud in the form of brick, called the Court House." The men drank whiskey, chewed tobacco, and played games while waiting for the court to open. They

wore bearskin caps, Mackinaw blankets, leather leggings, and carried "old Bess rifles and hunting knives."

Court sessions were frequently informal. Sometimes they were adjourned for a buffalo hunt or they might be speeded up to allow the judge and the lawyers to pitch quoits.

For the farmer, the once-a-week trip to town for supplies was a holiday, while townsfolk enjoyed a hayride into the country and a picnic by a stream. The twenty-five cents a young man paid for such a jaunt was cheerfully spent because of the "cuddlin'" that was permitted as the hayriders journeyed home after sundown.

In more elevated environments, there were singing schools and dancing academies. Dancing masters often were intriguingly French; singing teachers were more likely American but attractive nonetheless. Emerson gave benign approval to singing and dancing as "civilizing" enterprises. Others athirst for culture learned to play violin, harp, or flute, or joined debating clubs and literary societies to test the effectiveness of their elocution lessons.

Certain holidays were best celebrated in towns. The Fourth of July, for

111

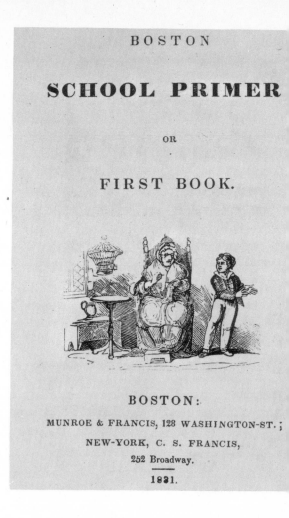

one. In 1826, the fiftieth birthday of the nation was everywhere celebrated with special fervor. Veterans of the Revolution had a particular place of honor in the great jubilee. Thomas Jefferson, too ill to attend the ceremonies at Washington (he and John Adams died that day), sent a letter in which he summed up the meaning of the Revolution for all to contemplate: "The general spread of the light of science has already laid open to every view the palpable truth, that the mass of mankind has not been born with saddles on their backs, nor a favored few, booted and spurred, ready to ride them legitimately, by the grace of God. These are grounds of hope for others; for ourselves, let the annual return of this day forever refresh our recollections of these rights, and an undiminished devotion to them."

Towns across the country continued down the years to refresh memories. The firing of salutes was a regular part of the fun. The shots and the brass band terrified the horses and caused runaways that in turn frightened spectators. Firecrackers prolonged the din after the parade had ended and the band music was stilled, after the picnic in the grove had stuffed everyone to satiety. Shirt-sleeved patriots orating on the bandstand outdid themselves on this day. Toasts were flowery: "The ballot box and the cartridge box—the former powerful in expressing, the latter in defending, the will of republicans."

The Fourth was not the only occasion when towns paid tribute to the men who had used the cartridge box effectively. Decoration Day was especially moving because the parade that began at Monument Square included many Civil War veterans—men who held the town's youngsters spellbound with memories of battles and the crash of musket fire. Nearly every town had its cast-iron monument to those who had been killed in action.

Recreation for village children was
likely to be more complex than that of their country counterparts.
Instead of whittling under a
tree, they could usually be found busy at street games,
or exploring the intracacies of store-bought toys.

Wives of veterans had their own vivid memories. The playing of the "Star-Spangled Banner" recalled for them days when the national anthem was played not only by bands but "whistled by juveniles, sung in the theatres —sentimentally lisped at every piano by patriotic young ladies, ground out on church organs, hammered on tin pans by small boys. . . ."

"John Brown's Body" had been the northern going-away song. The women left at home sewed clothing for the volunteers. A group of feminine patriots "manned" their town's cannon one fine day and fired a thirty-four-gun salute. A woman treasured the daguerreotype that her soldier boy had posed for before going off to war. Johnny Reb marched off to the tune of "Maryland, My Maryland." ("The despot's heel is on thy shore!" wrung the hearts of southerners.)

Hundreds of Billy Yanks remained in Dixie after war's end to marry and live in the South, leaving sweethearts, (or even wives), at home to eat their hearts out with jealousy. To these forgotten women the old wartime songs brought especially bitter memories. "Yankee Doodle," "Battle Cry of Freedom," "When This Cruel War is Over"—such songs they might still be able to bear. But what happened when the band turned the pages of the popular song books to "The Girl I Left Behind Me" or "Weeping Sad and Lonely"? Were their sagging spirits just a little bolstered by the devil-may-care tune of the soldiers' favorite, "Let the Wide World Wag as It Will, I'll Be Gay and Happy Still"?

Yet spirits rallied—and holiday or no, the band played on. Towns took great pride in their bands. Saturday concerts in the park provided sociability of a summer's evening. Citizens contributed money to supply the colorful uniforms that were as important as the instruments.

*The village blacksmith
was an important figure in the
community. The old saying
that your horse's feet were no better than
your blacksmith, indicated the
high regard for a good craftsman.*

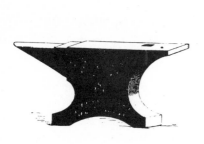

Fancy uniforms were also the hallmark of the volunteer fire department. The firemen were lionized because they came dashing to the rescue whenever the alarm rang. And they were equally ready to do the town proud in a parade.

The greatest show, however, was the circus. For generations, circus trains criss-crossed the back country bringing an outrageously wonderful world of color and excitement for hard-working people to marvel at. The circus was a national institution, eagerly awaited each spring.

"A Brilliant, Gorgeous, Imposing and Magnificent Living Panorama, Resplendent with Glitter and Gold," promised a poster. And every word was true, and became truer in memory in the monochrome days after the circus departed. "Sixty cages of Wild Animals, Huge Massive Chariots and Golden Tableau Cars. 5 Elephants in Harness, 10 Dromedaries, Zebras and Camels in Harness"—the creatures were bizarre, but harness these people knew about—. "Also the Gorgeous Moving Temple of Juno, 30 feet high, with the living Elephant Topsy, only 38 inches high, on the Top of the same; a Genuine Steam Piano"—that was the calliope—"Three separate and distinct Bands of Music, forming Altogether the Most Imposing, Brilliant and Grand Street Procession ever Witnessed."

People converged on the town early in the morning of a circus day to watch the tents going up. Before noon they had taken all available space along Main Street to wait for the parade. Finally, drums were heard in the distance and pulse beats quickened. Richly dressed drivers snapped their whips over the heads of the prancing white horses pulling the gilded circus wagons. Aboard the bandwagons, brightly uniformed musicians blared marches with an irresistible beat and brassy songs sublimely gay. The cheering throng fell in behind the whooping calliope that ended the procession and followed it to the big tent. Indulging themselves shamelessly with peanuts, they waited in transports of pleasure for the grand march to begin.

The greatest showman of his day was Connecticut's P. T. Barnum, a shrewd and knowing man who compounded out of the inexpressible longings of small-town people a show that lifted the heart, while frazzling the nerves, and survives even today with its ritual format virtually unchanged.

Before his time, the menagerie was the big attraction and a tavern's barn served as the big top. Here might be shown a lion or a camel, a giraffe or an orangutan, to an audience that had paid twenty-five or fifty cents to see the exotic beasts. Barnum himself had an "Asiatic Caravan, Museum and Circus" that boasted the "Largest Menagerie in the United States," plus General Tom Thumb, "Smallest Lilliputian in the World," who regaled audiences by riding a baby elephant.

Buffalo Bill's Wild West Show crowded them in to see elephants, leopards, kangaroos, and the many other strange creatures that had boarded Noah's ark. Added attractions were human freaks—Siamese twins, living skeletons, and bearded ladies. The great thrill came when the Deadwood coach was attacked by wild Indians.

While the circus had to keep piling thrill upon thrill with ever more daring acrobats, bareback riders, and more spectacular "spectacles," the "Uncle Tom's Cabin" troupes never had to change a line to move audiences to tears. But even they competed with each other in offering "embellishments" in the form of bloodhounds and jubilee singers.

Another popular attraction was the "Museum," which featured wax figures of famous people and "Panoramas" of well-known battlefields in all their gory detail. "Museums" also offered lectures on phrenology. "Dr. Cranium" was one of the first to lecture on this new and fascinating "science" that measured personality by the shape of the head. For twenty years many other "professors" continued these lectures. More amusing were the popular demonstrations of nitrous oxide—"laughing gas." The pleasant sensations it produced resembled intoxication—"an irresistible propensity to laugh, dance and sing . . ." The town's lyceum gave lectures on mesmerism, animal magnetism, natural history, chemistry, and astronomy. Science—spurious or real—was new and exciting to wide-eyed audiences.

Americans would try anything. They were optimists and believed with all their hearts that their communities were destined for a brilliant future. They leveled the critics, the carpers, and the malcontents with heavy Nineteenth Century scorn: "Lay down your hammer, and pick up a horn!" "Go ahead!" was a national slogan. The country was full of hustlers—boosters, they were called later—fellows always working on some project to increase the size and prosperity of their town.

Once-quiet villages began to order their lives by the factory whistle. Berlin introduced tinware that became a fad wherever Connecticut peddlers carried it. When the nearby market was flooded with all the tin cups and saucers, plates, sconces and candlesticks, pails and milk pans that could be sold, the glib salesmen went far afield in wagons loaded to the top and with pails hanging all around. These banged together merrily through New England, all the way south to Georgia and west to the Mississippi.

As more big factories were built, their owners began searching for workers. Large wagons were sent out to tour the rural areas and recruit "hands."

Young girls were favored, but men, women, and children were all given jobs. Immigrants arrived from overseas and found their first jobs in the factories.

Factories inaugurated new ideas in building. They required lots of space, floors strong enough to hold heavy, steam-powered machinery, plenty of light, and no ornamentation. Engineers, not architects, planned the buildings to meet these specifications and they were functional in the extreme.

The factory became one of the most typically American of all our buildings. The log cabin had come from Sweden, the state capitols and the big public buildings had copied Roman or Greek models. California showed a Spanish influence, New Orleans was a mixture of Spanish and French. Gothic style had its vogue (some folks "Gothicked" up their old houses). But the unadorned, immensely practical factories that sprang up all over the country were purely American. They were not only built by hustlers, they were filled with immigrant workers who had come to the New World to hustle and make good in a land of opportunity.

In the West, the rivalry between growing communities was intense. Every inducement was made to get new settlers and increase the population. Native Americans were appealed to in newspaper advertisements. In mid-century the State of Wisconsin had an agent in New York City to find prospective homesteaders among the immigrants entering the port.

A desire for neighbors, for stores, schools, and services were all part of the drive. No less important was the hope of selling high-priced lots from acreage that had cost the original settlers little. Then they could move farther west,

The rewards—and the dangers—of
whaling were great. New Bedford at one time had three-hundred-and-thirty
whalers sailing the oceans. Men were often
lost on a cruise, and the homecoming was anxiously awaited

The resourceful seaport towns of the East lent
their ships to the western movement. The hopeful passengers avoided the
rigors of the overland trail, but would have a perilous
voyage around stormy Cape Horn before they made a landfall—and a
new life—in awakening California.

buy another piece of land cheap, and begin all over again to reap real-estate profits, as well as crops.

The appeal was attractive to young and restless Americans who believed in the promise of the new country. A son, tired of the old man's tyranny—and tired of following a plow and horse—might look for adventure along with land. For the self-reliant there was always the wilderness to tame. The backwoodsman chopped trees and made a clearing for his hut, with poisonous snakes and prowling animals for company. But his nerve was keen, his spirits high. "I'm a ring-tailed roarer!" the pioneer bragged. "I'm a regular tornado, tough as hickory and long winded as a nor'wester. I can strike a blow like a falling tree!" Jumping high in the air and kicking his heels together, he was "gamecock of the wilderness," ever ready to "rassle" an opponent or shoot a wild beast. If part of this was braggadocio, he was still a man to conjure with, a man who could feed, house, and clothe himself from the natural resources of the forest.

For much of early America, the evolution of a meaningful society awaited stable transportation. Only when people and products and information had quicker access to the isolated settlements could normality and refinement hasten their growth. This was particularly true as the nation moved west, but even along the eastern seaboard new routes were blazed wherever there was a dollar to be earned, adventure to be found, or true union of the states to be established.

In Colonial days, Americans traveled overland on foot or horseback, using Indian trails in the forests. Eventually, trees were felled and the trails through the forests were widened. Stumps and roots, however, were left to jolt the small carts that bounced along, straining wheels, axles, and the driver's good nature. Later, logs were laid side by side to form a corduroy road which offered a surface little better than the ruts and mud holes they covered.

The early stagecoach had no springs and to be a passenger in one for any distance was punishing. Some considered a carriage suspended on leather straps to be an improvement. But most travelers felt the queasiness caused by the swaying to be worse than the banging of their bones. Overturnings were commonplace and even an uneventful ride was made depressing by the green gloom of the forest. Overhanging branches of great trees allowed only slivers of sunlight to break through.

Gay, lusty wagoners dispelled the weariness of the road. With strong lungs and leathery hands they guided the powerful six-horse teams that pulled bright red and blue wagons through Pennsylvania. These were shaped like a dory, with high prow and stern to keep the load from spilling on hills. The wagon-bed could be detached from the wheels for use as a boat at river crossings. For protection against the weather it was covered by a tunnel tent stretched on hickory bows. This was the Conestoga wagon.

At taverns called "wagon stands," wagoners rested after their day's run. In the assembly room they played practical jokes on one another, smoked four-for-a-penny cigars ('stogies), and drank much whiskey at three cents a glass. They roared their way through an evening of song and dance. When they were exhausted they unrolled their beds before the barroom fire, and side by side, with their feet toward the blaze, they slept.

Conestoga wagons, in trains half a mile long, made a brilliant caravan along a busy road. Large wheels rumbling, bells jangling, canvas top swaying, these land frigates covered America's vastness.

Increasing traffic demanded better highways. New roads, called turnpikes (a pike placed across the road was turned when the toll was paid), were built by private corporations. So fast were they built that within a few years a stagecoach could carry its passengers from the East to the Indiana border in about two weeks, at a fare of five cents a mile.

The stagecoach driver enjoyed a loftier status than the wagoner. Along the route, he was recognized by all as an important personage. His passengers considered him captain; many famous travelers on the Cumberland or National Road treated him as a friend. He was a carrier of news. The arrival

Southern festivals were brightened
by the costumes and brassy music of Negro marching bands, while
city children in the North were entranced by
peep shows and other portable,
curbside entertainment. More elaborate diversion
could be found in the theaters and opera houses. In the concert halls
audiences thrilled to the voice of Jenny Lind.

121

Nothing equalled the excitement the circus
brought to town. For generations
circus trains criss-crossed the back country, bringing an outrageously
wonderful world of color and enchantment for
hard-working people to marvel at. It was a national
institution, eagerly awaited each spring.

of the coach brought excitement to all the communities along the way. At night the fine horses were cared for in stables instead of being left in the yard, and the driver was served five-cent whiskey instead of the three-cent variety the wagoner was accustomed to.

The stage driver covered twenty miles a day to the wagoner's fifteen. His vehicle was the express, the Conestoga the freight. Relay stations were twelve miles apart. The stage arrived full speed, the driver threw down the reins to waiting grooms, and then caught the reins of the four-horse team they were backing into the traces. The change, accomplished in a flash, fascinated small boys who dreamed of becoming drivers themselves.

On main roads, there might be fifteen coaches going east and fifteen west each day, repeating their fascinating performance at the way points to the delight of all who kept track of their regular schedules. Townsfolk knew their names and were on hand to watch for the arrival of coaches belonging to the June Bug Line, the Shake Gut Line, or some other favorite.

Innkeepers along the way often were former wagoners or stagecoach drivers. "Mine host" was known for his good cheer, which was as much appreciated by local people as by travelers from afar. He was always ready to pass along the latest news with the food and drink he provided. While he dispensed spirits at the bar, his wife prepared meals in the adjoining room and his daughters or a local wench served.

A loud bell or blast on a cow horn summoned the guests to meals and awakened them at three a.m. to resume the journey. Breakfast and supper were fifty cents each, dinner was a dollar for all the food you could eat.

A traveler in Illinois in the early days was delighted to come to Mr. Bull's hotel, "standing upon the bleak and timberless prairie." It was a three-room frame house. Its stove, full of coal dug from a surface vein in his garden, had overheated the place. The guest seated himself and finally the host appeared with "two free and independent citizens" (not servants, but "helps") who sat around the stove with him. They were engrossed in politics. Then Mrs. Bull called from the kitchen: "You John Bull! Stop that nonsense about old Zack Taylor, and come to your supper . . . The hominy's spilin'."

The traveler was pleased with the fried hominy, venison steak, and hot coffee which he ate in company with the hosts, their sons and daughters, and the "helps." Before bedtime, Mrs. Bull prepared "a strengthening draught" of whiskey and boiling water, to which she added maple syrup, nutmeg, and a dash of rum. After one glassful the guest felt a slight flush and listened to the family's stories with pleasure until he retired to the bedroom he shared with the three sons.

Most roads in the spring were almost impassable. Even on a main street in early Chicago, a stagecoach was mired in the mud for several days, so deeply that a sign was placed alongside it: "No bottom here." A traveler in the West remarked that "if the mud does not get quite over boot tops when you sit in the saddle they call it a middling good road." A Virginian in Ohio traveled in a stagecoach that was "neither wind nor watertight" but fortunately had holes in the floor to let the water run out. The road passed through forests where blazed trees indicated the route. Where the blazes forked, the driver often lost his way, finding it again only after a detour

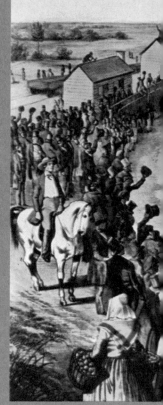

People were always ready to back
a champion—and to bet on him. Sporting
contests not only provided a
good show, but also the chance to make a little
easy money—if you were lucky.
Less formal than the prize fight or the horse
race, the turkey shoot was open
to anyone who could handle a rifle.

"over roots and stumps, across creeks and swamps, up hill and down."

In the distant West, over the long stretch from Missouri to California, the Federal Government lent aid to transportation companies to carry freight, mail, and passengers. The largest freighting outfit was Russell, Majors and Waddell, with headquarters at Leavenworth, Kansas. There great mounds of merchandise were piled into waiting wagons ready for the long pull to the Pacific Coast. On the eve of the Civil War, the company employed 4,000 men and 40,000 oxen to move its 3,500 covered wagons. Army posts, mining camps, and almost every other community in the trans-Mississippi West depended for their supplies on Russell, Majors and Waddell.

To hurry passengers and mail across the vast plains, the Overland Mail Company was formed by two experienced expressmen, John Butterfield and William Fargo. From Tipton, Missouri, where the railroad ended, the route bent southward across Texas, then through New Mexico and Arizona, and on into California. With loud hurrahs the first stages initiated the service on September 15, 1858, one leaving the eastern terminal and another the western terminal at the same time. In twenty-four days each had finished its 2,800-mile run. After that, strongly built, green and yellow Concord coaches raced regularly over the plains and deserts. Galloping horses kept them close to schedule, two each week in each direction. Snows in mountain passes delayed them, marauding Apaches and Comanches harried them. But the stagecoach usually got through.

The stagecoach was dramatic, but it remained for the Pony Express to make the mail carrier a national hero. Early in 1860, plans were announced for an express service to rush the mail across the plains and mountains from Missouri to the Pacific. The gallant Pony Express was under way on April 3, with the dispatch of a rider from St. Joseph, where the mail line ended, to San Francisco, about 2,000 miles away.

Each rider, spurring his Indian pony, covered his allotted stage—forty to

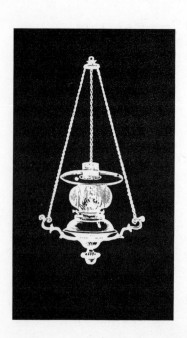

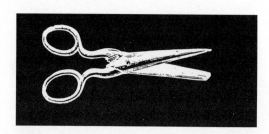

Prescriptions Carefully Compounded.

one-hundred-and-twenty-five miles—and then passed on his mailbags to the next man, who was away in less than two minutes. "No matter what time of the day or night his watch came on," wrote Mark Twain, "and no matter whether it was winter or summer, raining, snowing, hailing, or sleeting, or whether his 'beat' was a level straight road or a crazy trail over mountain crags and precipices, or whether it led through peaceful regions or regions that swarmed with hostile Indians, he must be always ready to leap into the saddle and be off like the wind." With a bite of bread and a gulp of water the rider was gone. The mails went through in eleven days, less than half the time of the fastest stagecoach. By a special effort, Lincoln's first inaugural was sped across in seven days, seven hours. Only one pouch was ever lost.

The Pony Express was a glamorous effort, but a financial failure. Even had it been successful it was doomed by the silent wires of the telegraph which flashed messages faster than the flying hoofs of ponies. But the Pony Express, during the eighteen months of its operation, gave to the nation an indelible memory of dash and courage.

Development of the waterways also put vast territories into touch with each other. Nature had been generous. The nation was knitted together by dozens of great streams, lakes, and bays. All that was required were bold men to learn the subtleties of navigating them, and terminals that would accept the cargoes of finished goods going inland and the rude riches of the hinterland outward bound.

Where waterways were lacking, canals were dug. The first major effort was the Erie, begun on Independence Day, 1817. Ingenious Yankee engineers utilized new devices to speed the task, but still they needed great numbers of men for manual labor. Irish immigrants, wearing long flannel shirts and slouch caps, worked up to their knees in the muck. In October, 1819, on a fifteen-mile stretch between Utica and Rome, the first barge made the first trip on the canal. "It was drag'd by a single horse, trotting on the embank-

The barber shop mixed the odor of cigars with the scent of bay rum and tonic.

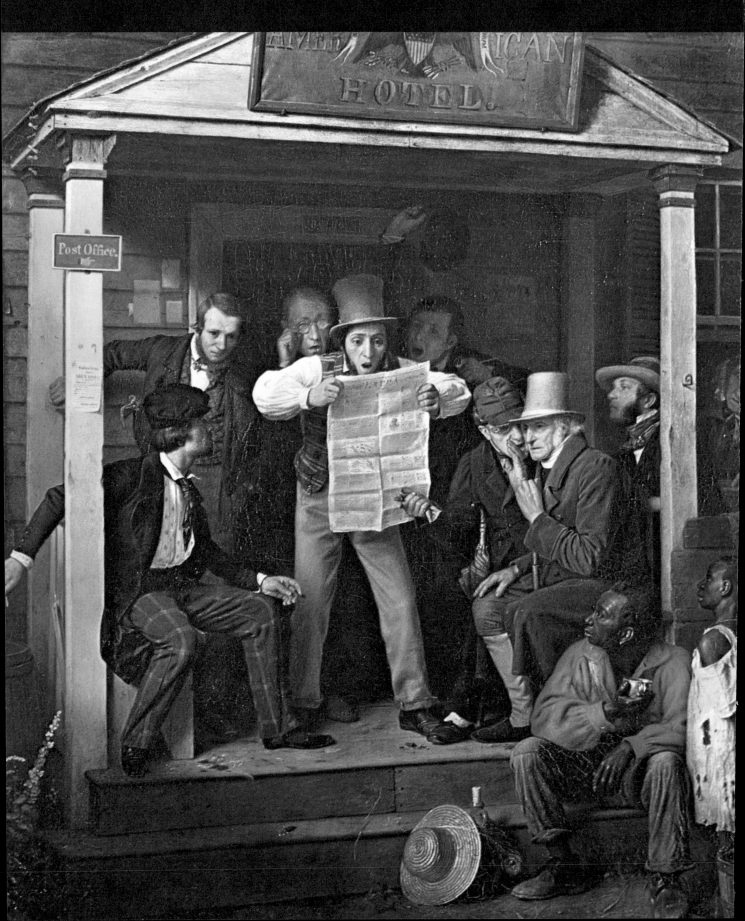

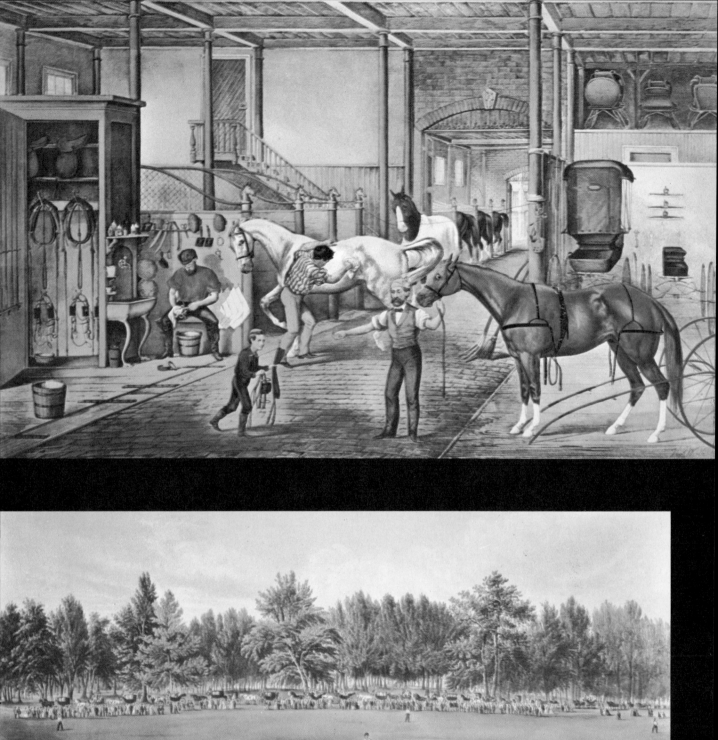

The mining town that sprang

up overnight was a strange conglomeration of people of all

nationalities, and peculiar

buildings flung together from any available material.

ment in the towpath . . . The embarkation took place amid the ringing of bells, the roaring of cannon, and the loud acclamations of thousands of spectators . . . who lined the banks of the new created river."

The whole country awaited each new section of the canal. Finally, after eight years, the entire route to Lake Erie was open. In late October, 1825, a flotilla of western canal boats with gay celebrants aboard sailed through the entire waterway to the Hudson, and then down the river to New York City, where thousands cheered them. Crowds along the banks, merrymakers in escorting boats, and the firing of guns celebrated the "wedding of the waters" as Governor De Witt Clinton poured kegs of water from Lake Erie into New York Bay.

The original Erie Canal, with its many locks, was three-hundred-and-sixty-three miles long, forty feet wide, and four feet deep. It cost over $7,000,000, but it gave a great boost to the country's business and paid off its debt within a few years. In 1826, when it was barely a year old, a town along the way counted 19,000 boats passing. The towpath was constantly busy; we "set sail by horsepower," said the boatmen. From Buffalo to New York the time for transporting freight was cut from twenty days to six, the cost from $100 a ton to $10.

Immigrants from Europe going West crowded the canal boats. The fare was about a cent a mile. There were usually twice as many passengers as berths, forcing the rest to sleep on the floor or on tables. Low bridges were a hazard to the unwary. The helmsman cried out, "Bridge" or "*Very* low bridge" to warn passengers to crouch. For a traveler who had missed the boat, the low bridge was a convenience. He could run down the towpath to the bridge ahead and jump aboard the slow-moving craft. As boats approached a lock there was a continuous blowing of trumpets and horns.

Men who worked and lived on the canal—"Canawlers"—have become part of our folklore:

> *We were forty miles from Albany,*
> *Forget it I never shall*
> *What a terrible storm we had one night*
> *On the E-ri-e Canal.*
>
> *Oh the E-ri-e was a-rising,*
> *The gin was getting low;*
> *And I scarcely think we'll get a drink*
> *Till we get to Buffalo.*
>
> *We were loaded down with barley,*
> *We were chuck up full of rye;*
> *And the Captain he looked down at me*
> *With his goddam wicked eye.*
>
> *Oh, the girls are in the Police Gazette,*
> *The crew are all in jail;*
> *I'm the only living sea-cook's son*
> *That's left to tell the tale.*

Many states were stirred to feverish canal building of their own. Some ditches were successful, but millions of dollars were poured into others that could not possibly pay off.

None was more bizarre than Pennsylvania's effort to make boats climb mountains to get to Pittsburgh. Canal boats were taken apart in sections (the passengers remaining in them, however), then placed on railroad cars to be carried on inclined planes over the 2,300-foot crest of the Alleghenies for a distance of thirty-six-and-a-half miles. At Johnstown the craft were reassembled at the Canal and the traveler continued on his way toward Pittsburgh. The canal ran on a stone aqueduct and then into a tunnel through the mountain. It was all very ingenious, but not profitable.

Rivermen were an even lustier breed than the "Canawlers." They boasted, "No one can do as the boatman can, the boatman dance and the boatman sing, the boatman is up to everything." Mark Twain knew them as heavy drinkers, tough fighters, profane, bankrupt at the end of the trip, great braggarts, yet generally honest and trustworthy. Mike Fink was thought to be the greatest of rivermen. He said so himself. He boasted he could out-run, out-jump, "out-brag, out-drink an' out-fight, rough-an'-tumble, no holts barred" any man on the river from Pittsburgh to New Orleans.

The professional boatman's costume was his trademark. A bright red flannel shirt was covered by a loose-fitting blue coat (a jerkin) reaching to his hips. His trousers were brown linsey-woolsey. He wore a coonskin cap and moccasins, and a hunting knife and tobacco pouch in his belt. His speech was as vivid as his dress. To describe something that happened fast the boatman said it was "quicker nor a alligator can chaw a puppy." His warning yell of danger ahead was "Hell's a-snortin'!"

All sorts of craft rode the western rivers. Where there was no stream, said westerners, boats could be made with a draft so shallow as to float on a heavy dew. Flatboats took about six weeks to float downriver from Pittsburgh to New Orleans. They, too, were commonly used by westbound emigrants. The unwieldy craft was a "mixture of log cabin, fort, floating barnyard and country grocery." They were fitted with loopholes for firing rifles when Indians attacked from the riverbanks.

When the steamboats came America's inland waters were transformed. John Fitch, Oliver Evans, and others had been tinkering successfully with steamboats for years before Robert Fulton's *Clermont* wheezed and coughed its way up the Hudson, in August, 1807. Fulton's was the first really practical boat and it revolutionized transportation. It moved at about five miles an hour and the round trip between New York and Albany took four-and-a-half days. In place of masts the strange craft had smoke stacks. In place of spars, rigging, and sails it had a walking-beam, pistons, and huge paddle wheels. Some few onlookers saw it as a sea-monster breathing fire, but they were sensibly ignored. Within a few years steamboats appeared everywhere on America's lakes and rivers.

The size and luxury of their steamboats was a source of pride to Americans, the more so because traveling Europeans were so amazed and impressed. Fulton's own *Paragon,* which succeeded the *Clermont,* had a large dining saloon seating a hundred and fifty persons. A Russian visitor expressed astonishment at its "gleaming silver and bronze, shining mirrors, and mahogany." Its wines were choice and ice cream was served in summer. "It is," he said enraptured, "a whole floating town!"

Each new steamboat on the Hudson tried to surpass its predecessors in size and splendor. The *S.S. Drew* was as sumptuous as a European palace, with woodwork in white and gold, rich carpeting, ornate chandeliers, and a magnificent "grand stairway." These boats could make more than twenty miles an hour, although they risked explosion in trying for speed records.

Steamboats on the Great Lakes and western rivers, carrying freight as well

After church on Sunday, the
weekly social calls were paid. Ladies could compare
recipes and admire new bits of finery
while their men waited patiently or warmed themselves before
visiting the next neighbor's house. The
winter holidays meant it was time for the traditional
raffle for the plump Christmas goose.

as passengers, cut the keelboat's thirty-day trip from Louisville to New Orleans to one week, the return, upstream, from ninety days to sixteen.

The first steamer on Lake Erie was the *Walk-in-the-Water,* which sailed between Buffalo and Detroit in 1818. While she steamed through the Detroit River, hundreds of Indians stood on the banks transfixed by the sight. They understood that the white man had a ship drawn by sturgeon, and here it was, right before their eyes.

Steamboats burned wood. On the Mississippi they stopped to load up twice a day. The captain blew the boat's whistle to notify the woodcutter along the bank that he was coming in for "wooding up." At night, blazing pine knots threw a red glare over the scene. "A few minutes of mad labor sufficed to cover the boat's spare deck-room—the torch is quenched, and with a jerk of the bell, the steamer moves off into the darkness."

Half-sunken trees, floating islands, rapids, floods, and frequent changes in the river bed made the Mississippi a severe test of a pilot's skill. To be a pilot, said Mark Twain, "a man had got to learn more than any one ought to be allowed to know; and . . . he must learn it all over again in a different way every twenty-four hours."

While pilots worked, passengers enjoyed the scenery, played cards, threw dice, drank, and flirted. A proud western journalist said that easterners, who called "us . . . backwoodsmen, would not believe that such fancy structures of oriental gorgeousness . . . [were] rushing down the Mississippi . . . or plowing up between the forests, and walking against the mighty current." A steamboat coming up from New Orleans "brings to the remotest villages . . . and the very doors of the cabins, a little of Paris, a section of Broadway."

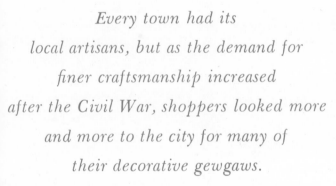

*Every town had its
local artisans, but as the demand for
finer craftsmanship increased
after the Civil War, shoppers looked more
and more to the city for many of
their decorative gewgaws.*

Steamboats competed feverishly. The most exciting event on the river was a race between two well-known rivals. Since it was publicized far in advance, spectators came from distant points to line the riverbanks and cheer their favorites on. Perhaps the most famous of all Mississippi races was won by the *Robert E. Lee* over the *Natchez*—up from New Orleans to St. Louis in three days, eighteen hours, and thirty minutes.

The rivers also enabled entertainment of unimaginable splendor to reach the towns along the banks and the backwoods communities beyond. This glorious treat was the showboat. In the early days the town crier was hired to go through the streets announcing that the showboat had tied up at the dock and would give a free concert and performance at seven-thirty at night. The coming of steam made things even more exciting. Instead of a theater drifting down river on a barge, the specially built, elaborately decorated showboat was towed by a little steamboat. On the hurricane deck was a "steam piano," a calliope!

This wonderful instrument could be heard five miles away, whistling a familiar tune to announce its coming. The sound of "Old Kentucky Home," "O, Dem Golden Slippers," or "Dixie" piercing a mist over the river, brought folks to a halt, to listen enthralled. Busy hands stopped rubbing at the wash-tub in the back yard, or hoeing a potato patch. Many a listener could recognize his favorite calliope player. "Crazy Ray" and "Calliope Red" were famous.

The showboat tied up at the river landings for a one-night stand and left before dawn the next morning on the next twenty-mile journey for a new audience. Actors in the East quickly learned of these audiences hungry for entertainment. Nothing could appeal more to an actor. And a trip to the exciting West held a special lure.

Of course, there were dangers to be faced: river pirates, riverbank cave-ins, and floating logs that could sink a boat. Greedy town officials sometimes charged exorbitant license fees. Occasionally, the husky bouncer had to subdue a rowdy patron. But as a rule the audiences were orderly, and the actors, many of them gifted artists, gave their best, whether in comedy, melodrama, or adaptations of Shakespeare.

The coming of a showboat was a happy occasion when old friends met to enjoy the theater together. Families came in their buggies or boats from miles away. It was a very mixed group that sat down on the hard benches at curtain time: poor whites and plantation owners, mine owners and foundry

Magazines and newspapers contained a multitude of

advertisements proclaiming the virtues of some highly dubious

products. Others, of course, did pretty

much what they said they would and achieved lasting

popularity. Lydia E. Pinkham, by far the best

known of the patent-medicine manufacturers, performed a

real service through her realistic advice to women.

Shoes no longer were
the ugly, uncomfortable, strictly
functional boots required by
the farmer, so skill and imagination were
asked of the shoemaker. Fine leathers,
bright colors and trimmings
adorned the feet of smart townspeople.

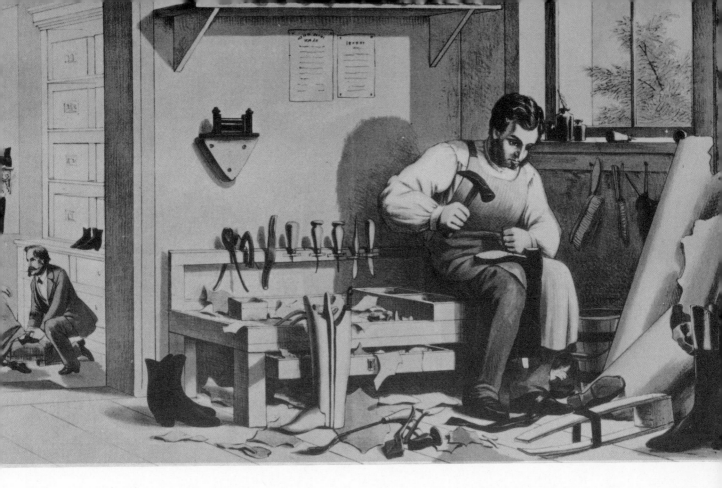

workers. All along the river, young and old came to enjoy a bit of glamor, to learn the latest catchy song and be dazzled by the bright lights.

The successful showboater included something for every taste. Captain French was one of the beloved showmen. Every evening he made a "Thank you" speech before the last act, and after the performance he shook hands with each patron. He and his wife were friends with them all and knew what they wanted. Their boat, *The New Sensation,* could be counted on for good, wholesome fun. It had more than twenty acts in its repertoire.

Usually, it began with a free show outdoors. Mrs. French (Aunt Callie to all) made up as a silly old lady, teetered on a tightrope high above the deck, while she sang the songs they loved. The show on the stage inside opened with minstrels in blackface who told jokes and danced. It then went on to acrobats, orchestra numbers, and magic tricks. At the end came a farce, usually "The Lying Valet," that had parts for the whole cast.

In later years Captain Price's boat, *The Greater New York,* had a huge success with "Ten Nights in a Bar Room." The death of angel-faced little Mary at the hands of her drunken father brought tears from audiences all along the rivers and bayous.

The various routes for showboats converged at Paducah, at the juncture of the Ohio and the Tennessee rivers. Its "duck's-nest harbor" offered a haven, a place to gather in February and March to prepare for the spring season ahead. Here rivals met and some boats changed hands. Captain Price, after a quarter of a century, was at the height of his career, with a fleet of four famous showboats.

Rivalry was keen. At one time Captain French found that having a photographer on board helped business. For twenty-five cents the river people could have tintype likenesses of themselves that were as good as the ones townsfolk got in a regular studio.

Showboaters knew that audiences did not vary greatly. The minstrel shows and circus were sure-fire hits on the river as well as in towns. Even strait-laced churchgoers accepted the amusing antics of blackfaced comedians.

The minstrel show had two parts. First came the jokes and songs that ended with a "Walk Around" leading to the wings. The second half brought on the stars with their banjo solos, duets, or quartets, dancing and sketches. Billy Conway, comedian, or Willie Guy, song and dance man, were famous. So was Hank Mudge, the country's champion clog dancer. A colored banjoist, Horace Weston, became world-famous. Larry and Billy Freeze were the champion "tambourine spinners of the world." Al G. Fields' minstrels were popular in the Midwest for more than twenty-five years.

Although steamboats were supplanting flatboats, keelboats, and rafts on American lakes and rivers, sail was still the queen of blue water. New England's port towns had been famous from the earliest days for ship-building, and the vessels that left from Salem, New Bedford, Nantucket, Mystic, New London, and the rest, brought back fabulous cargoes of whale oil, sealskins, fish, and the bartered goods of distant places. American captains brought ivory and gold from Africa, coffee and palm oil from Arabia, tea, pepper, and silk from the Far East.

Placid village streets and stores were
attractive places for citizens to while away an
idle hour, speculating about newcomers
in the area, perhaps evaluating the attributes of a comely
young lady shopper passing by.
An old-world art produced uniquely beautiful American glassware.

All these and more were taken in exchange for New England brick, hides, onions, salt beef, and rum. Ginseng root, which grew wild on American soil, was called the "dose of immortality" in the Orient and was worth its weight in gold. Even New England ice was traded profitably in the West Indies, once the Yankees learned how to insulate it for the voyage.

People in New England's ports mentioned remote areas as casually as though they were neighboring towns. An English visitor was impressed by the wild tales of young captains who had been to Mozambique and Madagascar, to Canton and the Sandwich Isles. They "touch at the ports of Brazil and Guiana," he said, "look about them in the West Indies, feeling there at home; and land, some fair morning—and walk home as if they had done nothing very remarkable."

The sealers left from New Haven where, early in the Nineteenth Century, the famous Long Wharf was built to accommodate them. Sealskins added great revenue to the already rich trade with the Orient—and a heavy stench to the air. The green was covered with thousands of skins set out to dry in the sun and the scent that hung in the air was more pungent than the onion smell of Wethersfield.

Equally aromatic and infinitely more profitable was whaling. So great were the returns that whalers went to sea from Long Island Sound and even inland river ports as far north as Poughkeepsie. The paramount whaling town, however, was New Bedford which, on the eve of the Civil War, had a fleet of three hundred and thirty whalers cruising the Pacific, the South Atlantic, the Indian Ocean, and the China Sea.

*Newspapers were widely
read throughout the country, practically
every county seat having
two weeklies to reflect the views
of the major parties.*

A ship might be gone for several years. Farmers near a port prospered because of the food supplies needed for the long voyage. Countless barrels of beef, pork, flour, molasses, and dried beans and peas came in farm wagons to be loaded onto ships. A whaler returned with banners waving in the wind, as if in response to the waving of the crowds on the docks and the roaring of the welcoming cannon. Along with the rejoicing there was always a note of sadness because some men very likely had been lost on the voyage.

But in the hold were barrels of oil for lamps, spermaceti (taken from the whale's head) for fine candles, and whalebone for corsets. If the cruise had been a lucky one, there was also rare ambergris, found only in sick whales, which was used in the making of perfume.

Eventually, the kerosene lamp and the electric light would replace the oil and the candles, and new fashions would supplant the corset. By the end of the Civil War, whaling was greatly diminished.

The swiftest ships in the world were the slim, beautiful clippers, unbeatable in a race for China's tea or around the Horn to bring treasure-seekers to California's gold fields. But they, too, were short-lived. Steam power would do them in.

The ships that ran to San Francisco during the Gold Rush risked losing crews to the mining towns that sprouted overnight. The New York *Tribune* had sent a reporter to San Francisco because its readers, like people everywhere, were eager for news of California's excitement. He described the town's appearance at night as "unlike anything I ever beheld. The houses are mostly of canvas, which is made transparent by the lamps within, and transforms them, in the darkness, to dwellings of solid light. Seated on the slopes of its three hills, the tents pitched among the chaparral to the very summits, it gleams like an amphitheater of fire. Here and there shine out brilliant points, from the decoy lamps of the gambling houses; and through the indistinct murmur of the streets comes by fits the sound of music from their hot and crowded precincts."

The greatest crowd was at the Eldorado. "There are about eight tables in the room, all of which are thronged; copper-hued Kanakas, Mexicans rolled in their sarapes and Peruvians thrust through their ponchos, stand shoulder to shoulder with the brown and bearded American miners." At one end of the room was a large bar, "and in a sort of gallery," a girl played the violin "to minister to the excitement of play." The place, the reporter said, was "rank with tobacco-smoke, and filled with a feverish, stifling heat, which communicates an unhealthy glow to the faces of the players."

Rich Bar, on the Feather River, was a typical mining town with one street and one hotel. The forty houses were made of rags, canvas, logs, or

Even bigger than the Gold Rush

was the boom created by the discovery of oil—first in

Pennsylvania, then in many other states. Wherever

a successful well was dug, tents and shanties immediately

mushroomed. These temporary quarters were

replaced shortly by a town with streets, frame houses,

stores, restaurants, and land offices.

To Miss Drusilla Clarke.

AMERICAN PETROLEUM

This oil well threw pure oil 100 feet high.

This oil well is now flowing 355 Barrels daily.

LITH. OF HENRY C. ENG 57 PARK ROW NEW YORK.

The above Photographic View of the Tarr Farm Oil Creek Pa. was kindly furnished by Wed W. Clarke & Co 10 Pine Str. N.Y.

Entered according to act of Congress A.D. 1864, by W.T. Hall in the Clerks Office of the District Court of the United States, for the Southern District of New York.

POLKA, SCHOTTISCH, GALOP, WALTZ, MARCH.

BY

J. J. WATSON,

NEW YORK,

Published by Wm Hall & Son, 543 Broadway.

New Haven
Skinner & Sperry.
Pittsburgh,
Wamelink & Barr.

Rochester,
W.S. Mackie & Son.

Buffalo,
Penn & Remington
Chicago,
Alanson Reed.

145

Coal and steel, the bulwarks of
America's economic structure, drew thousands of toilers
to the sites of their mines and mills.

planks. The inhabitants, again, were a mixture of nationalities. All told, there were five women among them; they were treated most respectfully by the men. The two-story hotel was "fitted up with that eternal calico, which flushed the whole social life of the 'Golden State' with its everlasting red." One large room served as a bar and a shop where miners bought their clothes and groceries. The parlor was in the rear, and boasted a straw carpet, a fourteen-foot sofa, red calico curtains, a cookstove, a table, and a rocking chair. Upstairs were several bedrooms with red curtains against purple walls. The crude building with its warped floors had cost $8,000.

A cultivated New England woman, living in a log cabin with her doctor-husband in 1851, described Rich Bar's celebration of Christmas. The hotel had been newly redecorated with red calico and vast quantities of brandy and champagne had been brought in. As a concession to the season, the floor had been washed! The festivities began with an oyster and champagne supper, with songs and toasts. Dancing (men with men, because of the woman short-

age) lasted throughout the next morning. Heavy drinking went on for three days. No man was allowed to abstain, until they were all on the floor, howling.

In Sacramento, crowds of miners filled a theater three times a week. "The canvas building," said the *Tribune* man, "fronted on the levee. . . . It would have been taken for any ordinary drinking house, but for the sign, 'Eagle Theatre,' which was nailed to the top of the canvas frame. . . . The prices of admission . . . box $3, pit, $2. The spectators are dressed in heavy overcoats and felt hats, with boots reaching to the knees. . . . The sides and roof of the theatre are canvas, which, when wet, effectually prevents ventilation, and renders the atmosphere hot and stifling. Several acts [of the play] are filled with the usual amount of fighting . . . Mrs. Ray rushes in and throws herself into an attitude in the middle of the stage: why she does it no one can tell. This movement which she repeats several times in the course of the first three acts has no connection with the tragedy; it is evidently introduced for the purpose of showing the audience that there is,

147

actually, a female performer. The miners, to whom the sight of a woman is not a frequent occurrence, are delighted with these passages and applaud vehemently."

The Golconda that outshone even gold, however, was oil. It would be found eventually in California and bring another generation of boom-town speculators charging westward with a glint of riches in the eye. But it was first discovered in Pennsylvania, and the rush to capitalize on "black gold" in the staid and settled East was every bit as feverish as that of the forty-niners.

Titusville was where it all began. Edwin L. Drake, a retired railroad conductor and semi-invalid, was the man who started it.

It was not his own idea. He was not a hustler with a hunch. He simply met a man at his hotel who was interested in promoting the Seneca Oil Company. Drake was induced to invest his savings in the company and act as its general agent. He was sent to Titusville where oil had been oozing out of the ground for years without arousing much interest. Folks had smeared it on aching muscles or on horses to keep flies away, and a few companies had been extracting "coal oil" from oily shale. But until promoters sniffed the possibility of cheap, volume production, no one had bothered much with it.

The promoters hired Drake to dig for oil, and it was this inexperienced man who floundered for a year on what all the locals considered a thoroughly silly

project. He had trouble getting hired help, or even tools. But, finally, he found a driller he could rely upon, and at sixty-nine feet they hit a gusher.

Titusville grew famous overnight. Stock of the Seneca Oil Company rose spectacularly in value and farmers along Oil Creek were offered fabulous prices for their land, or even for leases on their land. Derricks sprouted up. A local shoemaker, who owned land but had no money for machinery, "kicked down" a well and struck oil at eighty feet. His homemade machine was worked by foot power, but his well was successful enough to bring him more than four hundred gallons a day—and crowds of sightseers. The local blacksmith dug an even deeper well, which yielded four gallons a minute.

The tidy white houses of the prim village were suddenly surrounded by a shanty town. The wooden sidewalks were crowded with boomers and big-city slickers. The streets were filled with shouting teamsters hauling barrels of oil to the railroad or to the barges on the creek. Although Drake made little money for himself, many a poor farmer realized a sizable fortune and many a sucker bought stock in dry wells.

Toward the end of the century, oil became one of the nation's basic industries and wildcat drilling spread to many states. Wherever a successful well was dug, tents and shanties immediately mushroomed. But within a few months these temporary quarters were replaced by a town with streets

By the 1870's, the newly rich American was discovering that the country highway was not only the fundamental link between boroughs, but also a very agreeable avenue on which to display himself and his grand equipage.

149

and frame houses, stores, restaurants, saloons, and land offices. The local post office was deluged with mail. Then, if earth's riches ran out, the excitement faded, people left, and all that remained was a ghost town.

Kerosene was the prime product; the automobile had not yet begun to gulp gas. Gasoline was at first discarded. Later, it was used in the manufacture of varnish, oilcloth, and patent leather. Another by-product was paraffin for making candles and topping jelly glasses. Various oils were used for lubricating steam engines and other machinery, as well as the axles of horsecars. People were quick to see the convenience of oil for bright lamps and stoves that cooked food without overheating the kitchen. The demand for oil exceeded the speed and capacity of surface transportation, and the pipeline was developed. In 1879, a hundred-and-ten-mile pipeline from a field in western Pennsylvania allowed the oil to flow underground to a railhead. By the Eighties they were being installed at a furious rate. "Tong gangs" used huge tongs to lay eighteen-foot sections of six-inch pipe in a ditch.

In the last decades of the century the town was in transition. It would not lose its rural character completely; it would always have an element of innocence that the more cynical city lacked. But more and more, the products, fashions, and mannerisms of the city would find their way to Main Street. The townsman acquired the new-fangled automobile just as quickly as the

The village shopkeeper now took the
train, or drove over the rural roads, to the big city
for his association's annual convention. During
the year, he kept in touch with innovations in his field through
the salesmen or peddlers who called
on him. Sometimes he took the whole family to visit one
of the natural wonders of the country.

Society was intent on preserving

the unity of the family, whether in work or at play. Girls

were taught to emulate their

mothers, to learn the wifely duties they would

later assume. Boys were encouraged

to follow in their father's

footsteps. Togetherness was not the exception.

urbanite. The telephone, the telegraph, the growing network of highways all bound the town closer to the sources of action and inspiration. It was a flourishing period for newspapers, too. The impact of events was swiftly felt in towns everywhere.

Yet physically the town would retain for many years its more leisurely pace and more intimate sense of involvement in its people's lives. The town would always know, for instance, that the large glass bottle or bright-colored liquid in the drugstore window attracted various customers, not at all interested in buying medicine. Where busybodies watched with narrowed eye to see who was pushing through the swinging doors of a saloon, a man was safer going to the drugstore for a "prescription." Several barrels of wine and whiskey were always kept to treat "sore throats."

The wide assortment of popular patent medicines in many cases owed their success to a shockingly high alcoholic content. Other of these "absolutely harmless" nostrums contained opium and promised—truthfully enough—to pacify the most fretful child. By the 1880's there was an endless variety of "sarsaparillas" and "celery tonics" that cheered while they cured.

153

The popular press helped to skyrocket sales. Newspaper and magazine ads were far more effective than signs painted on the side of a barn. Women, lonely and worn out with much child bearing, suffered from "female complaints" and needed "nerve tonics." Lydia Pinkham was only one of hundreds of manufacturers of patent medicines, but by far the best known.

She offered not only a "cure-all," but a sixty-page "Guide for Women" that became so popular it eventually was printed in five languages. Thousands of letters came to her which she answered with sage advice, serving as the chief "psychiatrist" of her day. She was not only wise and kind, but was also very clear in explaining the functions of the body without a false sense of shame. There were many questions about their personal lives that women needed desperately to have answered. Lydia Pinkham answered them frankly and in strict confidence.

While a drugstore's large stock of patent medicines offered comfort to the ailing, its soda fountain offered sociability and refreshment, especially for the young folk. Here they came to meet their friends and "suck an ice cream soda"—even on Sunday. Drugstores were permitted to remain open on the Sabbath, but clergymen and other influential citizens complained that they abused the privilege by serving sodas. The practice was condemned in sermons and finally forbidden by special ordinance. To evade the law drugstores then served ice cream *without* soda, but with a liberal addition of syrup, nuts, and fruits. These concoctions were called "sundaes" in mock deference to the lawmakers.

Shops specializing in these refreshments were known as ice-cream parlors. Some were elaborate establishments with rooms reserved for ladies and their escorts. During a hot spell they were the most popular spots in town. Flirtations were carried on while the milk shakes and floats were being prepared.

Drugstores could satisfy a mild craving for alcohol with their patent medicines and prescriptions. While the "Peruna drunk" went to the druggist, the serious drinker headed for the saloon. Saloons were fitted up with long, brightly polished counters. Behind the bar glittered a huge mirror reflecting the sparkling array of glassware and whiskey bottles. On the walls hung pictures of fighters and race horses. Oil paintings of voluptuous nudes gazed calmly from gilded frames at the roisterers at the bar.

The saloon, however humble, offered sociability—and free lunch with every nickel glass of beer. On the buffet were cold cuts, pickled pigs' feet, hard-boiled eggs, and cheese, along with sliced rye and white bread.

Once mass production and
distribution had been firmly established, goods were available
to everyone and the formation of a
middle class and an elite became possible. With
prosperity came refinements, both in material possessions and in
social graces. Women were able to make the
home a gentle place; entertainment in the front parlor had
about it an air at once convivial and polite.

155

Saloons were the targets of temperance people, including the town's newspaper editor, although town gossip had it that he didn't mind taking a nip or two himself.

Newspapers were widely read throughout the country, practically every county seat having two weeklies, one for each of the political parties. Politics, reported in strongly partisan language, local news, and items about former residents who had removed to other communities, were printed in the columns of these papers.

The kind of gossip that filled the air around the stove in the general store was also printed for all the community to read. In the spring a paper would report that everyone was busy cleaning out stovepipes and emptying cellars of rotten fruits and vegetables. In time, national and international news stories supplied by large city papers were added to this staple fare.

Editors in an earlier day depended on official patronage—the publication of land sales, tax lists, and such—to add to their income. Job printing, binding books, printing cards and Valentines, and selling magazines were all done by town editors. Subscribers often paid in produce, which was better than no payment at all.

Often the writing in the weekly paper was undistinguished and given to cliches. People did not dance, they "tripped the light fantastic." A new born male infant was invariably a "bouncing boy." Still, the editor was frequently a lively and progressive force in the community. He promoted cultural activities and often encouraged youthful literary talent.

And in such activities he epitomized and reflected the townsman's concern for his town. The town usually knew itself well and found its personality worth preserving. Its rectitude was sometimes burdensome, but its heart generally was warm. There were many things it did not approve of, or did not want to know about, and these, in time, would seem stifling to its young people and urge them to the cities where they could try to make a grander vision of life come true. But aspirations such as these could only come from an environment that respected the individual and usually, when the time came, let him go his own way.

Perhaps this accounted for the town's tolerance of eccentrics. There often were odd characters around town who were comfortably accepted as part of the familiar scene. First it was the itinerant peddler, whose manners and ways of life were alien, but who was welcomed nonetheless.

In rural areas the peddler, whatever his oddities, was respected as a much-traveled man of experience who brought news and offered counsel. In villages, the owner of a crossroads store played the role of learned adviser. In towns the storekeeper was the man of affairs enjoying contact with the

Americans were an energetic and

restless people, often seeking new challenges to meet.

Despite the efforts of the older folks to

maintain an undivided family, the time came for many a young man

when he struck out alone—perhaps to get a better

education, perhaps to make his fortune. No uncertainties he felt

were as strong as his desire for independence.

big city; drummers from afar came to call on him. The townsfolk had a good chance to study this glamorous type as he strutted around the New Main Hotel, with cigars in his vest pocket and his hat at a jaunty angle. The off-color jokes he told as he held court on the veranda, were quickly circulated.

The owner of the hardware store was not only friendly with the drummer, but he, himself, took an annual business trip to the city. The small-town storekeeper in the South was courted by the wholesaler in Louisville. "Merchants Associations" in "wholesale cities" held conventions and offered lavish hospitality and free entertainment to a storekeeper—making sure he went home with not only merchandise but fond memories. Both were of great interest to fellow townsmen when the storekeeper returned.

He might bring back a description of the Mammoth Cave that he had visited. Better than that, he now owned one of those new stereoscopes. With this gadget he could show pictures of famous scenic wonders that seemed so real you felt you were right there yourself. Soon he was buying those "double pictures" by the dozen to show his friends. Civil War battlefields, sentimental or humorous shots, some hand-tinted, were popular. Scenes of life in the big city were among the favorites.

The city was undeniably alluring. Even the townspeople going nowhere enjoyed strolling down Depot Street to the railroad station to watch the trains come in. The sight of a steam locomotive and its rattling chain of cars never lost its thrill. Often enough, the traffic was light: one or two passengers debarked, and one or two—perhaps the storekeeper off to a convention or the drummer on his way up the line—swung aboard. And perhaps there was some baggage or freight to be off-loaded.

But the excitement lay not only in the swish of steam and the clank of steel, but in the promise of what waited at the journey's end. Through the years, that distinctly American sound—the train whistle in the night— stirred the hearts and haunted the spirits of generations of youngsters lying a-bed in the upstairs rooms of little houses on the peaceful streets of American towns. For many of them, the sound would one day became irresistible and spur them to join the restless movement of Americans over the face of their land.

The character of the town would
remain essentially rural and attract those who craved
serenity. But the train whistle in the
night lured countless others to the congested city.

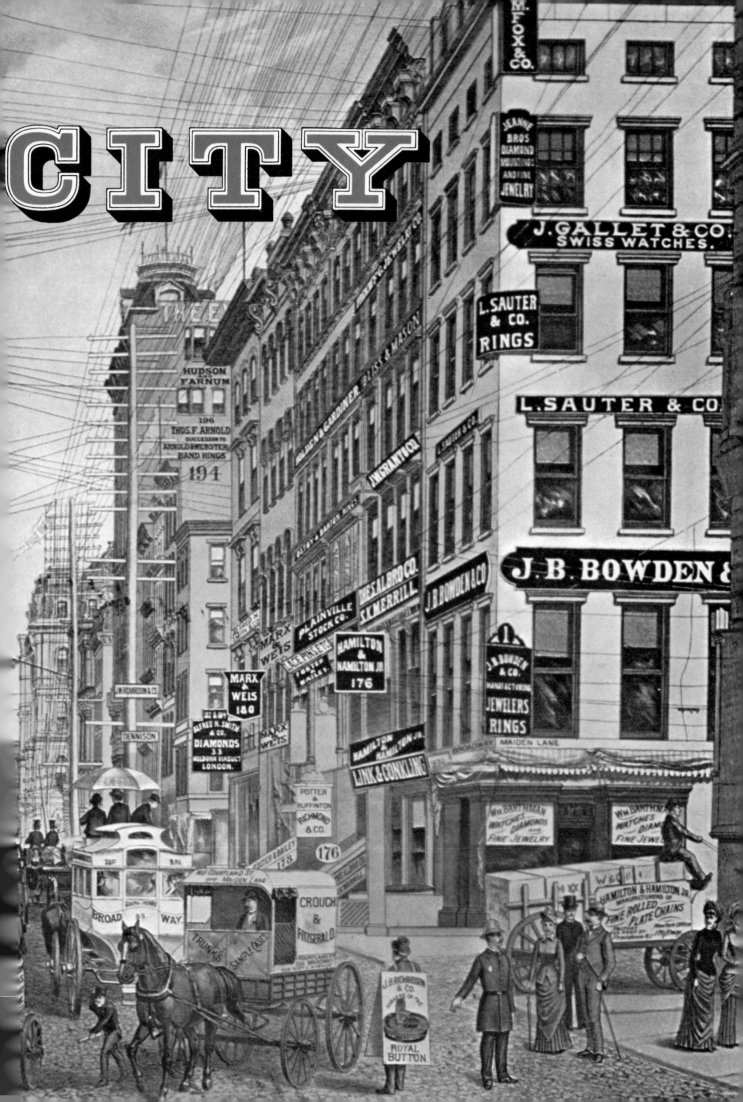

Davy Crockett was a brave man. He was not afraid to march straight up to a ferocious bear in the wilderness. But when he left for the big city he was less sure of himself. In his *Tour to the North and Down East,* he recalls his misgivings as he headed for Philadelphia: "I sort of felt lonesome as I went down to the steamboat. The idea of going among a new people, where there are tens of thousands who would pass me by, without knowing or caring who I was, who were all taken up with their own pleasure or with their own business, made me feel small. . . ."

"Tens of thousands"—more or less. A city was full of strangers no matter what the exact size of its population. This was one of the many things, some obvious, some subtle, that distinguished it from the country and the town. Away from the city people seemed more neighborly. Similar backgrounds and common problems led to friendliness. Self-interest prompted it also —one never knew who would need help next. The sick, the defeated, the bereaved—all depended on the assistance of neighbors, who gave with customary kindliness. But the city was strangers.

Yet the city was also excitement. It had the excitement of size, of diversity, and of important things happening. It covered more ground, had more and bigger buildings, offered more goods in the stores, more entertainment in the theaters. It had more churches, more schools, libraries, parks, museums, hospitals, hotels, restaurants, and taverns. It had more monuments, more lights, more noise, and more success. Altogether, its lures were powerful and attractive enough to make most people put aside and forget their timidity in going among strangers.

All of these sizes and numbers were relative. A city of pre-Civil War days might be no larger than a town today. It was not until the second decade of the Nineteenth Century that the United States had a city of 100,000 population, and not until the 1870's would it have one of a million. Still, small or large, the city had an atmosphere and temperament unique and inimitable. The city was a fount of power. It controlled money and, therefore, most of the things to spend it on. It offered fame and provided the admiring audience to give it zest. And, as town and country rarely did, it had a place for intellectual, non-physical work.

The big cities of the early days were Boston, New York, Philadelphia, Charleston, and New Orleans. Each had its style, its sophistication, that set it apart from the others and from the upstart towns in its sphere of influence. The best accounts of what they felt like are the journals of visitors, who came, with senses alert, to sample them. One such *tourista* was Anne Royall, who saw all the big cities of the Atlantic Coast between 1824 and 1829. She was immediately aware of the quotient of strangers in any city. "It is difficult for a stranger," she wrote," to decide upon the manners and appearance of any city or town for this reason, at least one half of the people he meets in the streets and public places, are [themselves] strangers. These are from the country, from other towns, other states. . . ." But, she concluded matter-of-factly, "this is what makes a city."

As she approached Boston by boat, it appeared to rise out of the water in great beauty. The dome of the State House, the cupolas of Faneuil Hall, and seventy white church-spires soaring above the pattern of roof tops impressed her greatly.

Close up, the city lost some of its lustre. She felt oppressed by the narrow, crooked streets with their borders of tall houses, some of them five stories high. She disapproved of the poorly paved and lighted sidewalks, and the carriages that thundered through them with the barest passage room on either

The city had the excitement of size,
of diversity, of important things happening. It covered more ground, had
more and bigger buildings, offered more goods, entertainment,
and facilities for education and health. It
was also a center of power and influence that radiated out over the country.
Its successful citizens carried the mark of assurance.

New York's Park Theatre,
the setting for many theatrical successes,
also saw the debut of grand
opera in 1825. Peaceful Savannah
would one day hear the tramp of Union
armies while northerners exulted.

Among the principal early cities were Boston and New York. The Boston Common and Broadway were famed—but quite dissimilar—landmarks for the European visitor to see. He was usually impressed.

side. She was surprised that the stores closed at dark; in New York and Philadelphia evening was the time young people liked to shop. By contrast with their lighted windows and lively streets, Boston seemed gloomy.

Yet this was the tide of progress. For thirty years, Boston had been undergoing a transformation. Dating from about the time of John Hancock's death in 1793, Boston's architects, led by Charles Bulfinch, had been altering the appearance of the city. The little white houses on tiny grass plots were giving way to taller buildings. The "Federal" style was imposing an ordered yet graceful formality that perfectly expressed the intellectual pride and conservatism of the city's leading residents. Some quaint, colonial charm was being lost and certain noisome aspects of the city were intruding, but the change was undeniable and much of it was for the better.

166

Mrs. Royall liked Beacon Street. Its homes were as lovely as any in the land. A portrait by Gilbert Stuart in a Bulfinch house was a combination she found quite irresistible.

Faneuil Hall blended idealism and utility; the "birthplace of American liberty" was, "and always has been, used as a market-house. It is open on all sides, and filled with butcher's meat." The market offered prime cuts, fresh vegetables, and live fish which swam for the buyer's inspection in tubs of salt water.

The Common had an air of permanence. For the yearly inaugural of the Governor it was packed with citizens come to observe the ceremony and listen to the fine municipal band. On summer evenings it attracted strollers. Merchants in scarlet coats and cocked hats promenaded sedately. Tight knee-

breeches and silver buckles were worn in Boston after they were no longer the fashion in other American cities. The salt breeze blew in off the sea and Mrs. Royall saw "the spruce beau, the pert apprentice, the statesman, and the beggar, all tread the mall in the pride of independence."

Evidence of culture delighted her. She commented favorably on the Athaeneum library of 19,000 volumes and on its collection of fine paintings and statuary. But she was an indefatigable reporter and she knew that the waterfront and the great brick wharves, four stories high and reaching more than a thousand feet into the water, were good, too. The shops sold rope and rum, loaf sugar, candles, glass, sailcloth, and beer—all Boston-made. But now that more people were becoming literate, symbolic signs—a shoe, a glove, a hat—were giving way to lettered ones.

The city's commerce was being surpassed in volume by New York's, but it was still the root of the fortunes that underwrote the many humanitarian enterprises of proper Bostonians. The Massachusetts General Hospital, the poorhouse, the penitentiary, the orphan asylums—all these represented the best impulses of the period. The ladies of Boston, although celebrated for their beauty, were most admired for their benevolence. Mrs. Royall praised them and so, later, did Charles Dickens, an expert on institutional life.

Davy Crockett, arriving in Boston a decade after Mrs. Royall, was most impressed by the city's school for the blind. He wanted to see the mills at Lowell, and did—"not because I had heard of 'the mile of gals' [tending the spindles]; but I wanted to see how it was that these northerners could buy our cotton, and carry it home, manufacture it, bring it back, and sell it for half nothing . . . and make money besides." On the other hand, he declined an invitation to visit Harvard, believing it would not suit his style.

Indeed, Harvard was not the place for a frontiersman. This was the time of Emerson, Hawthorne, and Thoreau; of Bancroft and Prescott, the great historians; of Horace Mann, who was reshaping the country's public schools; of William Ellery Channing, the world-renowned Unitarian preacher—all of them Harvard graduates, all of them among the brilliant minds of a brilliant era. Boston was unself-consciously proud of them, but, knowing itself to be the Hub, could hardly see how matters would stand otherwise. For more than half a century it would set the tone for the cultivated people of America and half persuade the British that Americans were civilized.

New York cared less for its past than Boston. Now recovering from the devastation of the war, it was striking out afresh with characteristic dynamism to become the city of superlatives. Its harbor was one of the finest in the world, with water deep enough to allow the largest ships to dock at shore line. The tall masts of sailing ships rose above the roof tops of the warehouses that stretched for a mile along the water's edge. Here were stored the imports and exports whose handling gave the city wealth.

In the period when Washington was inaugurated the city's population was 30,000 and crowded near the island's tip, favoring the East River side. Already it was a cosmopolitan city that mingled many peoples and many lan-

The city could support many small

specialty shops. The ultimate in high fashion was available

to society's grande dame, while attractive

but reasonable garb could be had by a lady less well-off.

169

An important businessman
could not afford to take the time to write his own
letters; he acquired a secretary,
perhaps a member of the family with inadequate means who was thus
able to earn her keep in a genteel manner.
An employment agency handled the requirements
of the businessman's wife—domestic help to take care of
her spacious flat or palatial town house.

guages, and it was confident of its capacity to absorb more. The imprint of the Dutch was evident: houses of yellow brick, churches, family and street names, words like "cookie" and "stoop." The English who followed were sensible fellows, quick to co-operate for commercial advantage in trade and land speculation. These two not only tolerated each other in business dealings, but also intermarried. Business and tolerance seemed to be ingrained characteristics of New York.

The Tontine Coffee House, built early in the 1790's on the northwest corner of Wall and Water streets, was the choice meeting place of businessmen. Already it was being used as an exchange for the bonds of the Government and the State. Fraunces Tavern, the New York terminus of the principal stage routes, was another meeting and eating place. In the summer months, gardens like the Vauxhall or the Ranelagh, near the Battery, were recreation centers for the entire community.

New York's streets, particularly Broadway and the Bowery, were wider and straighter than Boston's and traffic already was a problem. Congress complained that its deliberations at Federal Hall were unsettled "by the al-

*In 1811, when New York
was clustered mostly around her
harbor at the island's tip,
optimistic city fathers established a
gridiron pattern of streets
reaching almost to the city limits.*

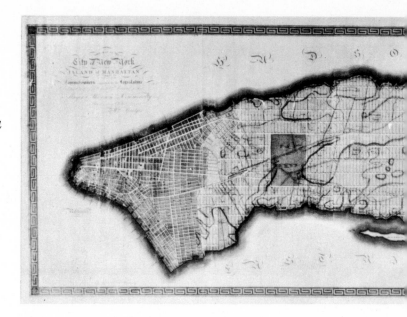

most unceasing noise of passing carriages." Traffic thereupon was banned from the precincts of Broad Street during congressional sessions, a stopgap, but not a solution. The clamor of the city would never abate.

Federal Hall was an architectural show place, and it had been hoped that the Federal Government would decide to make its permanent home there. But in the spring of 1790, it piled its documents and books and other belongings into some wagons and rumbled off to Philadelphia. Never again would it travel so lightly.

New York shrugged off the loss and went on about the business of becoming a great city. New parks were laid out, swamps drained, and trees planted. In 1811, the famous "gridiron" map was drawn and the future streets and avenues of the city were indicated to the northern limits of Manhattan Island. It was a far-reaching conception; the city was still confined largely to the lower tip of the island and the rolling acres of what one day would be uptown were dotted with handsome homes, well-sited on lovely country estates.

Not long after the War of 1812, New York had surpassed Philadelphia and became the nation's principal city. It was, a southern visitor said, "a life-inspiring city." "I never saw more industry, or more general application to business of every description . . . than in this city. Turn which way you will, mechanics, carvers, carpenters, bricklayers, ship-carpenters, cartmen, all is one continual bustle, from morning till ten o'clock at night. No wonder New York outstrips all her rivals."

The whole city was surrounded with masts and churning steamboats. The sounds of axes, saws, and hammers, the ring of the blacksmith's anvil, the "Jolly tar with his heave-ho," the noise of rattling carts, all contributed to the city's cacophonous chorus.

Much of it was raucous, but there was a pleasant lilt to the familiar cries of the vendors who moved through the streets selling bread or strawberries, buttermilk or yeast, charcoal or ice. The chimney sweep, the boot cleaner, and

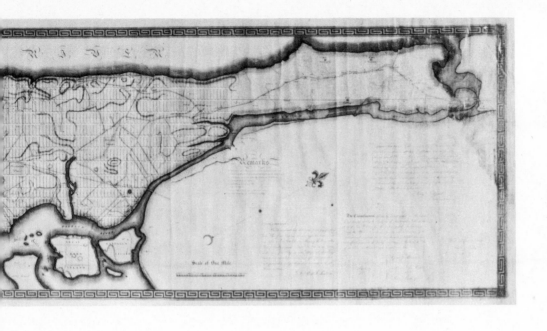

*The Tontine Coffee House, built in
the 1790's at the corners of Wall and Water Streets in New
York, was a favorite meeting
place and bond market for businessmen.*

the scissors grinder matched cries with the man whose pushcart supplied root beer at three cents a glass.

Famed Broadway in the 1820's was eighty feet wide and four miles long. Much of its sidewalk was paved with brick or flagstone, the roadway with cobblestone. But the thoroughfare was already too narrow for its traffic. At its lower end "the attempt at crossing is almost as much as your life is worth." Pedestrians were advised "to look up the street and down street" and then run for their lives. Broadway was noted for its appeal to the fashionable and gay. But there was a drawback to New York's charms. It was said to be the dirtiest city in the Union.

One of its compensating attractions was the theater. When President Washington lived in New York, he often went to the John Street Theatre, where he saw "The School for Scandal," "Conscious Lovers," and other plays presented by a repertory company. Washington's diary notes: "A good deal of company at the levee today. Went to the play in the evening. Sent tickets to the following ladies and gentlemen and invited them to take seats in my box. . . ." When it was announced that Washington was to attend a certain performance, the theater would be packed. Everyone applauded at the entrance of the President and "Washington's March" was called for.

In 1825, New York was given its first opera, "The Barber of Seville," at the Park Theatre. It was received with wild enthusiasm. Seven years later, the famous English actress, Fanny Kemble, appeared at the same theater; New Yorkers found her enchanting. Theater, in fact, was the city's chief entertainment and it was considered a pleasant diversion to visit Edward Windust's restaurant on Ann Street, to see the theatrical folk who gathered there. The actors congregated at a long table to eat steaks, be admired by their fans, and chat with the likes of Washington Irving, James Fenimore Cooper, and other literati.

The city's elite dined at the Astor House, which opened in the 1830's and quickly became the leading hotel of visiting celebrities. It was named after the country's richest man, John Jacob Astor, who owned fabulous amounts of New York real estate and was earnestly reported by gossips to be earning $5 a minute. His hostelry was flatly accounted "the eighth wonder of the world," and a southern visitor bracketed it in lofty company by proclaiming that "there is but one St. Paul's, one Niagara, one Astor House."

Sandy Welsh's place, in the basement of Barnum's American Museum, attracted the political crowd. Mayor Philip Hone was pleased to be greeted by General Tom Thumb, who was the Museum's main attraction.

Almost from the outset, New York was a trap for the unwary. Organized gambling flourished on Broadway. Ann Street, a magnet because of its theatrical associations, became the hangout of sharpers of every description, negligent, plausible fellows ever ready to fleece a mark. Pickpockets were rampant. Fake auction houses unloaded shoddy, or stolen goods, or were the scene of more elaborate swindles, and apparently did a thriving business

For a while, Baltimore was the country's
fastest growing city. Its bustling vitality contrasted strongly
with lush playgrounds like Saratoga Springs,
which attracted the moneyed city-dweller and rich
planters escaping the southern summer.

in spite of public notices—even men carrying placards—warning the stranger of their pitfalls.

City facilities were somewhat limited. The best drinking water in town came from the privately owned Tea Water Pump on Chatham Street; it cost a penny a gallon. The ordinary water from public wells had a peculiar taste and was always in short supply.

Water for fighting fires also was scanty. And since most of the city's build ings were of wood, and sparks from wood-burning stoves and fireplaces flew freely, the hazard of conflagration was great. Fire companies were manned by volunteers, each with its own spectacular uniform and brightly shining engine. The engines had pet names: Black Joke, White Ghost, Hay Wagon, Bean Soup, Shad Belly. And they were hauled through the streets on the run when the alarm sounded. Rivalry between the companies led to bitter disputes at the scene of many a fire. Sometimes "plug uglies" were hired to impede competing apparatus and allow another company to reach the blaze first. Sometimes there were brawls to decide who was going to do the job, and if the companies were evenly matched, a building could burn to the ground before the firemen could establish precedence for putting it out.

Before New York surged to the fore, Philadelphia, with a population of 42,000, was the country's largest city. Strangers easily found their way through the broad tree-lined streets, which were kept clean by the efforts of the first street-cleaning force in the nation. On the city's main thoroughfare the famous roofed-over market ran for nearly half a mile. Every Tuesday and Friday evening, the "butter bell" clanged out a reminder to get up early for market day. Before dawn, buyers would be on hand to get their butter, meat, and other supplies. The fame of Market Street (formerly High Street) spread so far that even towns without public markets gave the name to their own main streets.

Philadelphia had been greatly influenced by Benjamin Franklin, who pre-ferred it to his native Boston. The nation knew him best as the man who had brought lightning down on a string, and for *Poor Richard's Almanack,* but his colleagues in the cultural institutions of his adopted city were grateful for the importance he had brought to it. He was a man of great range, great style, and of wisdom made tolerable by wit. His funeral on April 21, 1790, was witnessed by 20,000 people.

Philadelphia, like New York and other growing ports, was beginning to see the arrival of thousands of foreigners, many of them Germans who decided to make the city their home. While a great number adopted Ameri-can ways and became assimilated into the city's life, there were groups, like the Amish and the Mennonites, that preferred to remain separate. They retained their native German in their church services and, like the Quakers, made a virtue of plain dress. Colors were drab and buckles and buttons were condemned as showy. Quaker men could be identified by their broad-brimmed hats, the women by the bonnets that were said to lend an attractive melancholy

Prosperous, beautiful, and

aristocratic, Charleston had a flavor mingling

France, England, and the West Indies. Its wealth came

from trade in rice, cotton, and indigo.

179

to their pale faces. Behind high walls, the Friends met quietly in their churches—"meetinghouses" that allowed no adornment or music.

As their men prospered, however, Quaker women rebelled against the traditionally somber fashions and started wearing the finest silks and satins. But they dressed only in white, which lent a somewhat celestial air to their appearance.

Pious, industrious, and humanitarian, Philadelphia was also the center of American science, art, and drama. Its Philosophical Society enjoyed world renown, its social life came close to equalling Europe's most sumptuous. Visitors were often shocked by the lavish display at some of the magnificent estates and "seats."

Those with a taste for luxurious living had managed to find outlets for it even under the British military regime. The redcoats gave a ball so splendid it went down in local history. Soon thereafter, however, there were beautiful American hostesses who proved themselves quite capable of providing their own memorable entertainment. The city's well-proportioned houses, as well as the elegant furniture in them, were the work of skilled native craftsmen who considered themselves the equal of foreign artisans. But European influences could still be felt. Titled French emigrés earning their living as dancing masters and booksellers may have added a bit of tone to the city.

While New York and Philadelphia had the stir and bustle of eastern commercial enterprise, Charleston had the mannered graciousness of a community certain in its own mind that it was unrivaled. Although not large—its population in the early Nineteenth Century was 16,000—it was extremely well-to-do from its trade in rice, cotton, and indigo. It had the flavor of France, of England, of the West Indies, and a Yankee traveler thought it "the most aristocratic city in the Union."

The heart of the city had fine, wide streets, with cool alleys connecting the back yards. The better homes, bright with pastel stucco and colored roof tiles, had courtyards and lush gardens perfumed with camellia and jasmine, and with fig, peach, and orange trees. Roses blossomed in February. Tea was served in the garden. People lounged on wrought-iron balconies or promenaded on the Battery at twilight. Elegant shops displayed the finest millinery and apparel to be found in America. Elegant homes contained the finest of furniture, silver, paintings, and books.

It was the planters' invariable routine to visit their estates, fifty miles or more from the city, in late fall, after the frost had lessened the danger of "country fever"—malaria. Christmas week was filled with a round of gay celebrations at the mansion, and then everyone returned to town to enjoy the "season" from January to March. Theater parties, concerts, dinners, and the ball of the famed St. Cecilia Society were on everyone's social calendar. The climax came with Race Week in February, followed by the Jockey Club ball, where guests danced until three in the morning.

At these times the city was riotous with silks and ribbons. Women were decked in ermine and point lace, in brocades and Indian cashmeres. They carried dainty parasols, or fans which they fluttered coquettishly. The men sported canes and "carried a trifle too much weight in the 'watch chain.'" Gentlemen who were accomplished amateurs in art and music gathered in one or another of the fine houses for congenial evenings of discussion and appreciation.

After the season, the rice planter went back to the country to stay until the ponds started to "green over." This was a sign of summer's heat and

Castle Garden was the scene of P.T.
Barnum's great triumph: his presentation for the first time in
America of the lovely Swedish soprano, Jenny Lind.

accompanying disease, and a retreat to the city—or even to northern resorts, such as Newport and Saratoga—was indicated.

A northerner visiting the South just before the Civil War said plantation owners were reluctant to keep their slaves in the cities. Working beside free Irish and German workmen "they get strange notions in their heads, and grow discontented." White girls were being hired more frequently as domestics. Skilled Negro craftsmen were let out to work in factories and were allowed to retain part of their earnings. From their savings, an increasing number of slaves was able to buy freedom. Some free Negroes managed to accumulate considerable property. In some instances, they were themselves slave-owners.

Queen city of the Mississippi was New Orleans, whose vigor and cosmo-

A taste for entertainment

on a lavish and spectacular scale swept the large cities.

Promoters competed feverishly to present "firsts."

politanism were a match for northern cities, and whose lack of inhibition was all its own. While it boasted a beautiful cathedral, people crowding into the square in front of it on a Sunday morning felt quite free to remain outside to watch the Creole regiment parading in full regalia to martial music.

The Sabbath was a day for recreation. Theaters were open. The coffeehouses were well patronized. At the coffeehouse one sipped hot punch, read newspapers, played dominoes, or sat in congenial company smoking a cigar. Faro and roulette were openly enjoyed by all classes from high noon until two in the morning when supper was served. A serious-minded New Englander was surprised that "the inhabitants have no fixed criterion of what is and what is not 'respectable.'"

On their day of rest, family men—their wives gaily bedecked in ribbons, scarfs, and feathers, and their children in tasseled caps—strolled along sidewalks that were thronged with sailors, planters, boatmen, priests, slaves, gendarmes, and soldiers. Those not strolling were looking down upon the crowds from their windows or balconies.

A long colonnade formed the market place. The large square fronting the river was bordered with retail shops selling wines, cigars, and dried fruits. The fanciest stores were in Chartres Street, the Broadway of New Orleans. Here were the cafés and confectioners, as well as bookstores, milliners, jewelers, dry-goods and perfume shops. After the evening gun roared over the city, the long avenues grew bright with lamps suspended by chains that stretched from house to house. Built of adobe, brick, or stucco, the

GRAND AEROSTATIC
ASCENSION,
OF CHARLES F. DURANT,

1st native citizen of the United States that ever attempted an Ascension in a Balloon, (Pup

*The wharves of the
steamship companies frequently were thronged
with excited crowds, sometimes
waiting to greet the next boatload of
immigrants, sometimes to bid
good-by to pioneers
sailing west, often just sight-seeing.*

houses were gaily colored. Beautiful wrought-iron graced balconies, gateways, and window gratings.

Here people with French, Spanish, and British ancestry had early become kin. To that mixture was later added the blood of newcomers—Irish, Germans, Italians. Free Negroes were prominent members of the community. Cultivated quadroons, educated in Paris, were a special, distinguishing feature of the city's life. Its manners, its music, its theater, its urbanity, its various languages gave it a European flavor. "We might . . . have fancied that we were approaching Paris," wrote an English visitor in 1846, "but for the Negroes and mulattoes, and the large verandahs reminding us that the windows required protection from the sun's heat."

On the levee that stretched for miles, steamers and ships of every description waited their turn to receive or discharge cargoes. Hundreds of flatboats and keelboats, manned by "Kentucks," "Buckeyes," and "Hooshers" from the upper Mississippi Valley, unloaded their horses, cattle, mules, and whiskey. With their profits the men took the homeward route as deck passengers aboard the palatial steamboats that were the river's pride. Bales upon bales of cotton were piled high on the levee for shipment to the North and across the Atlantic to Britain's textile mills.

Aboard a Mississippi steamboat were cotton planters in broad-brimmed, low-crowned hats. They wore their clothes, said a Yankee, "in a careless, half sailor-like, half gentleman-like air," with just a touch of the farmer. Among them was a Yankee lawyer, "in a plain, stiff, black coat, closely buttoned up to his chin, strait trousers, narrow hat, and gloves"—the direct opposite of the nonchalant southerners.

Up-river from New Orleans was St. Louis, which also possessed a special character. Mountain men, traders, and westbound emigrants made it their headquarters. Washington Irving noted its mixture of French and American customs, its French billiard room, its market place where French and English were spoken. From the upper Mississippi and from distant points along the Missouri came the furs brought in by colorful Indians and trappers.

St. Louis, "mistress of the western waters," had over 7,000 people in the 1830's. It grew rapidly in the following two decades, from river trade and the expansion of its surrounding region. Its population changed, too, when thousands of Germans came up the river, packed tight in the steamboats. They had been transferred from ocean-going cotton ships which had brought them from Europe.

A hundred steamboats were regularly counted on the levee, said a visitor in 1851, "taking in and discharging freight, letting off steam & pushing out or arriving. There is probably no busier scene in America in the same space. For two miles a forest of smoke stacks is seen towering above the 'arks' from which they seem to grow. All between this and the line of warehouses is filled with a dense mass of apparently inextricable confusion & bustle, noise & animation." Talk of business was constant. "Between fish and pudding," it was said, a speculator "will sell a prairie."

Rivalry among American cities was intense, particularly between St. Louis and Chicago. The former got an early start and, for a time, seemed well in the lead. With the coming of the railroads, Chicago's geographic position began to work in her favor and she rapidly drew ahead. Lacking even a

Perched high on hills above its magnificent bay, San Francisco was built with the gold from California's mines, the harvests of its golden fields, and the wealth of the railroads.

With the advent of the daily
newspaper, events were reported rapidly
to the whole country, in
language that was comprehensible
to everyone. *The N.Y.* Sun *was the first
successful penny-press paper.*

mile of railroad in 1850, Chicago in ten years was the center of eleven main lines and many branches. On the eve of the Civil War it had become the chief distribution hub of the West. But the beginnings some thirty years before were small.

The city began as Fort Dearborn in 1830. It was located on both sides of the Chicago River at the point where it emptied into Lake Michigan. It was primarily a defense post against Indian attack, but inevitably became a trading center, supplying salt, tea, coffee, sugar, and clothing to the back country. Even when it had no more than a hundred and fifty houses, it was infected with "growth fever." A Scottish visitor wrote in 1833 that almost everyone he met "regarded Chicago as the germ of an immense city." He noted that speculators had "already bought up, at high prices, all the building ground in the neighborhood."

Fifteen years later the city had 20,000 people, living in 3,000 small white houses. Sidewalks were of wood and the streets were covered by a plank road below which the undrained water stood stagnant. On the outskirts of town, roads often were quagmires. But with the pioneer instinct for putting the best foot forward, it planted its little plots with flowers and called itself "Garden City."

It became the center for farm machinery and home of the world's greatest grain market. Rivers of wheat and maize poured from its grain elevators. Steers that had walked to the railroad from Texas reached their destination in Chicago's odorous stockyards, and the processing of beef, pork, and lamb was also making the city the world's largest meat-packer.

Chicago was a transfer point for emigrants going to farmlands scattered over the western country. A visitor who saw men from Germany and Scandinavia passing through the city in 1848 spoke of them as "wild" and "rough," "their faces covered with grizzly beards." Sturdy wives and children were with them. "Neither cold nor storm stopped them in their journey to the promised land, on the frontiers of which they had now arrived."

Cities in the North and Midwest grew with frantic speed. Eating habits reflected the people's hurry. "Gobble, gulp and go" was the way a European described the American. His energy was boundless. He was "always working, building, starting afresh or beginning something new, always developing, extending himself or his country." In a land where equality was fixed ideal, and free education was intended to offer equal opportunity to all, success was the goal. A man was expected to succeed "on his own," without help from his father. As a result, competition was keen—"no holts barred." "Clever horse-trader" and "shrewd Yankee" were meant as compliments. If one "made good" in any field by his own efforts, he was in the tradition of the American success story. But no matter how successful one became, he was never supposed to look down on his fellow man. This was equality.

The growth of cities in the Nineteenth Century seemed spectacular because people could remember how small and how recent were the beginnings. Men lived into the Twentieth Century who could recall the small Chicago of their youth. Even when New York City had a fairly large population in the 1830's, it covered only a sixth of the island of Manhattan. Inhabitants of the denser part of the city lived within an area stretching across the island from river

189

to river, and north less than three miles from the Battery. The rest of the island was occupied by farmers and gardeners living in small villages—Yorkville, Harlem, Manhattanville. Many recent immigrants lived in "shanty towns" bordering more thickly settled areas. In these semirural surroundings they kept cows, pigs, goats, and chickens.

Change came quickly. In Chicago, in 1871, a visitor had seen within four years "wastes of sand and rubbish and weeds" transformed into "lovely public squares," the "comfortless shanties of the Irish immigrants" replaced by "beautiful and stately marble buildings." Nothing seemed stationary for long; houses were often moved, and cemeteries, too. Even the dead, it was remarked, "must 'move on' in Chicago."

The time of greatest expansion came after the 1860's. Then it was that cities lost much of the rural quality that had clung to them in their earlier years. A sharper distinction now existed between the sprawling large city and the smaller town. It was then that people spoke nostalgically of the intimacy of life in the town and village, a neighborliness that seemed to vanish in a city's anonymity.

As much as any other agency, the railroad helped to make the cities great. Although in one respect they laced the country together and brought innumerable small towns into contact with Metropolis, their ultimate effect was to accentuate the differences and widen the gaps that existed between urban and rural areas. For the volume of goods the railroad could carry and distribute gave tremendous impetus to industry. Countless manufacturers now had national outlets for products everyone seemed to need and the concentrations of wealth that poured in to them was reflected in the

190

Postal service improved, and
Samuel Morse made it
possible to contact distant
places by tapping a key.
Undersea cable
spanned the Atlantic in 1858.
President Buchanan and
Queen Victoria exchanged
messages. Broadway
gave the project a parade.

aggrandizement of the cities. More and larger factories serviced by more and more manpower sprang up at the terminals of the railroads, and this, in turn, meant booms in building and in providing goods and services for the swelling populations hired by business.

And all of this was set in motion in a matter of decades. With the development of efficient steam engines, it was inevitable that they would become a prime motive power. The charming, quite inadequate, horse-drawn railroad carriages quickly gave way to the locomotive. There was resistance at first. Turnpike operators and canal-barge companies were dead set against a swift means of transport. Owners of strategically located taverns bellowed at the thought of being by-passed. And fainthearted people in general viewed the coming thing with alarm. But the notion of a continent spanned by rails was too big to hold. By the Forties, resistance had faded or been overcome. By the time the Civil War approached, some thirty thousand miles of track had been laid.

Early trains inspired no confidence. Flying cinders threatened fire and boiler explosions were unnervingly frequent. To cushion against injury from collision, cotton bales were loaded on a car between the engine and the passengers. Engineering techniques were feeble. Bridges and trestles were insecure. But, as always, when an idea took hold, the improvements followed fast enough to clinch its place in the economy. The American genius was agreed to be mechanical and its energy unbounded. "We live for futurity,"

Vastly improved trains provided luxury travel over the old pioneer trails.

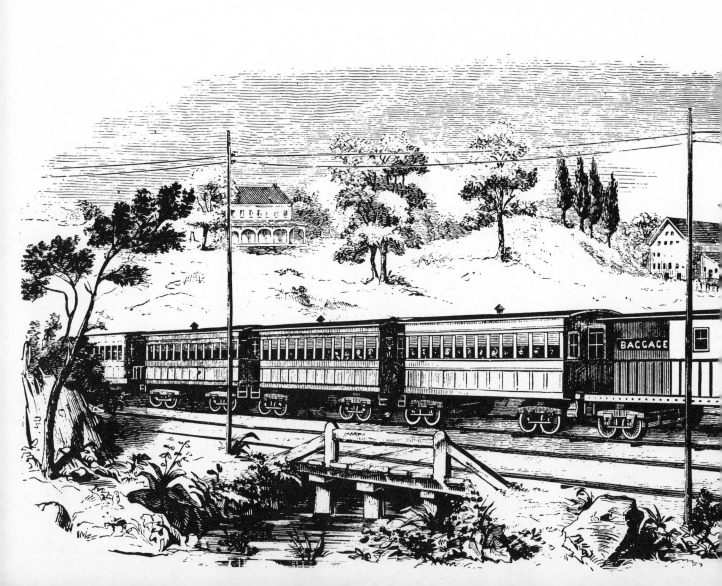

it was said, "and are doing the work of two generations yet unborn."

Engines became more powerful, rolling stock improved. Roadbeds were better graded and maintained. Signals, air brakes, fuels—all the accouterments of railroading became more efficient. And before long, the suspension bridge made it possible to span any river, chasm, or gorge in the country.

When California and Oregon entered the Union, the pressure for transcontinental lines was inexorable. Agitation grew for railroads to bind the coasts, and during the Civil War, Congress granted the assistance to make them a reality.

Surveys were made despite Indian attacks. Vast quantities of ties, rails, and spikes were hauled to Council Bluffs, Iowa, from where the Union Pacific would run west. The Central Pacific, mainly with Chinese laborers, started building eastward from Sacramento. When construction was well advanced, track was being laid at the rate of one to three miles a day. The greater the mileage, the greater the financial support and the larger the land grants from the Federal Government would be. In 1868, the Union Pacific proudly stated: "What the country has dreamed about for many years is becoming a reality." Early in May, 1869, only a few miles separated east and westbound construction crews. It was agreed that the meeting should be at Promontory Point, Utah, on May 10.

As the last few ties were laid (after an unexpected delay of three days), a space was left for the final one. It was made of California laurel-wood. The

ultimate rails were set and joined by a golden spike. Construction workers laughed in alcoholic glee when the honored guest tried to hit it and missed. "The last rail is laid! The last spike driven! The Pacific Railroad is completed!" wired the telegrapher on the scene. With gay ceremony the engineers brought "their locomotives face to face until they touched," each engineer breaking a bottle of champagne on the other's engine. The Atlantic and the Pacific, until then months apart, were now brought within days of each other.

More lines soon spanned the continent. Where the snows fell deep, vast sheds were built to cover the tracks to keep them open in winter. Tunnels were bored through mountains. Crack trains were fitted out with such luxuries as buffet, smoking, and library cars. Speeds increased to a mile a minute. To cities like Omaha the smoke of locomotives was as oxygen. They grew lusty on it, and the train whistle was music to their ears.

The nation's open spaces were being discovered and explored. Rivers, railroads, and highways made every place accessible. Only the remotest corners were beyond the reach of everyone. Now came the people.

Augmenting the native-born American was the immigrant. Throughout the Nineteenth Century, he came by the million. Some paused at New York, at Boston, or Philadelphia, but many went on to the farms and cities of the West. In the years before the Civil War, Irish and Germans outnumbered all other nationalities; by 1860 only Berlin and Vienna had more Germans than New York. In St. Louis, Cincinnati, and especially Milwaukee, the

In the North and Midwest,
cities like Cincinnati and Cleveland grew with
frantic speed and were fiercely
competitive. The surge of immigrants
augmented the native-born
population; in Cincinnati, German was more
often heard than English.

German language was heard in the streets more often even than English.

Irishmen, fleeing the potato famines of the homeland, clustered in the cities and sought work on the docks or on construction jobs. An Irish emigrant song described an America where:

> *They say there's bread and work for all,*
> *And the sun shines always there.*

After the Civil War, it was eastern and southern Europe, and Asia, that contributed most heavily to the immigrant tide. The bewildered strangers were bilked and swindled shamelessly, but the air was perfumed with freedom and opportunity and they breathed deeply. America! Businessmen were anxious to help you out with credit. "The politician" was ready to help you out if you got into trouble. Most important, you had a chance to work and better your life. Today you lived in a stifling tenement overrun

Milwaukee's industrious Germans

built a thriving metropolis; Nevada's Virginia City lived

high until the big veins—and the luck—ran out.

197

with rats and bugs, but tomorrow you might move to better quarters with running water and a private toilet. There was hope. Although newcomers clung to the language and customs of a lifetime, they were pleased to have their children go to public schools and become "Americanized."

Soon after the turn of the century the adults found a pleasant way to learn English and get a lesson in American manners. For five cents they could enjoy hours at the nickelodeon watching the flickering movies and the song slides. When the slide said, "All join in the chorus," they had a chance to try using the words they had learned. The settlement house was another place for foreigners to practice the new tongue and observe American ways. Certain phrases caught their fancy: "Ladies first" and "Time is money." These seemed to typify their new homeland.

Americans and aliens observed each other closely and absorbed each other's ways. Immigrants might continue to read newspapers in the language of the old country, but they learned to accept the dress and the habits and the marvels of the new. And brash America incorporated the speech and cuisine and talents of the newcomers into the amalgam of the free society.

The brawn of the immigrant helped build the waterworks, the sewers,

the streets, the streetcar lines, the tenements, and skyscrapers that gave the city its character.

The tall buildings were a wonder. As the price of city land increased, building outward had to stop and building upward was the only answer. New techniques made frame-steel construction possible and the invention of the elevator made the soaring shafts usable. "All's safe, gentlemen, all's safe," said Elisha Otis in 1854, as he proved the elevator to be practical.

Soon after the middle of the Nineteenth Century, the complex organization of city life demanded professional administration. Police and sanitation departments were established. Trained firemen took the place of brawling volunteers. The pig was banished from the city streets. Garbage scows carried the refuse of the gutters out to sea. A pure and consistent water supply was brought in by conduit from outlying reservoirs. Across the nation, the narrow brownstone houses of the city could now enjoy the luxury of running water; water closets instead of outhouses; stationary bathtubs and "rain baths" (showers) instead of bulky tin or wooden tubs. Central heating arrived, too. A furnace in the basement, stoked with coal, circulated hot air through pipes to registers in every room.

Colorful titles were bestowed on distinctive cities: New Orleans was "queen of the Mississippi," St. Louis "mistress of the western waters."

199

These brownstones were all alike. The front hall was the formal entrance. Its door had narrow windows on either side, so you could see who had pulled the handle that jangled the doorbell. Outside the door was a footscraper; inside an umbrella stand and hatrack, an elegant piece of furniture that also boasted a mirror and, altogether, was called a "hall tree."

The hall stairway, which encouraged banister sliding by the young, led to the bedrooms overhead. Each of these had a brass bed with fringed bedspread and, these days, closets instead of wardrobes. Another flight led to the attic—servants' quarters and storage room.

The front parlor had an ornate, straw-padded rug to keep feet warm. Lace curtains between heavy velvet draperies graced the windows. Wallpaper was flowery or scenic, the furniture carved and stiff. Thick portières hung at the sliding-door entrance. It was in this sanctum that a young lady entertained her beau. They sat on the horsehair couch with the silk cushions she had hand-painted, looking at stereo pictures, a book of engravings, or the plush-covered family album. Meanwhile, they nibbled the bonbons he had brought. She expected that fancy box of candy; he expected some of her homemade fudge. Occasionally, they went into the kitchen together to make taffy candy. This gave him a chance to put his arms around her. Candy and romance seemed to go together. It was as much a tradition as the chafing dish supper a young lady prepared for her escort when he brought her home from the theater—unless he had treated her to an oyster and champagne supper at a restaurant.

If they were not going out she might sit down at the upright piano and play for him. She had a large collection of bright-covered sheet music with which she entertained her swain. The popular songs were sentimental ballads that tore at the heartstrings: "Sweet Marie," "After the Ball," "Just Tell Them That You Saw Me," "Only a Bird in a Gilded Cage." If brother played the violin, it was his aim, too, to wring the heart. The rolls of the player piano presented music in the same style. The Regina music box on the table offered 1,000 different tunes, but none of them "snappy."

Lighting was revolutionized when smoky lamps were replaced by gaslights. The chandelier, high in the center of the room, was reached by a long gadget tipped with a slot for turning on the gas. A spaghetti-thin, lighted wax taper held by the same gadget was applied to the gas jet. Etched glass globes enhanced the light. Lights were put out when it was time for a magic-lantern show. Then a smoky little lamp sent its flickering light through the slide that cast a colored image onto a sheet that had been pinned to a wall in the children's playroom.

Although Americans relished the comforts of home, they were also attracted by the novelty of pleasure trips to distant places. Pioneers had shown the way. Now the tourists followed, in style. The railroads, eager for new sources of income, began building luxury hotels in the West to encourage the wealthy to travel at home instead of abroad. Hoping to cut into expan-

The inauguration of Jefferson Davis as President of the Confederacy at Montgomery, Alabama, crowned the division between North and South. The end of the war would see many changes for both antagonists.

200

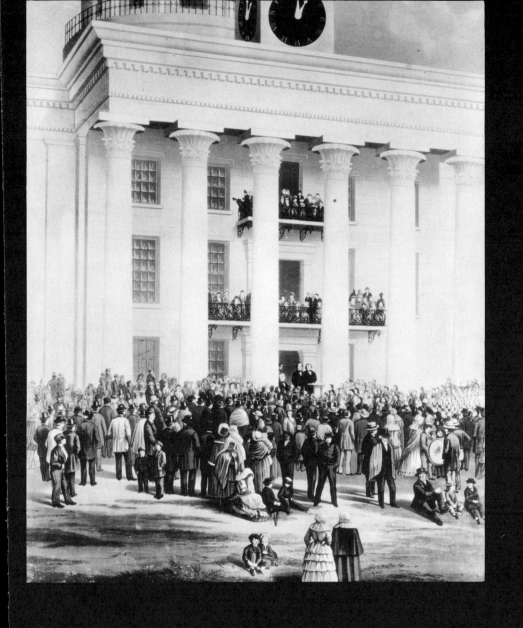

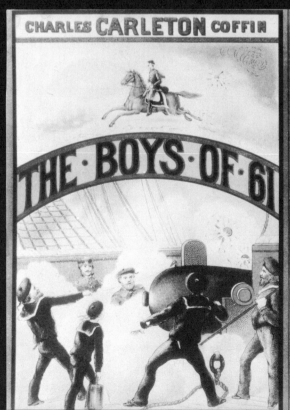

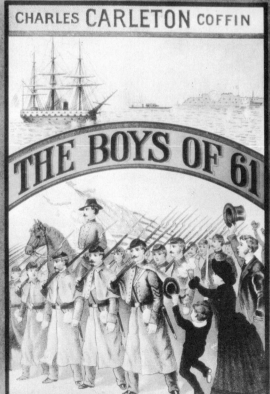

The infamous tragedy of
President Lincoln's death sounded a final note of bitterness
to the years that had torn the nation apart.

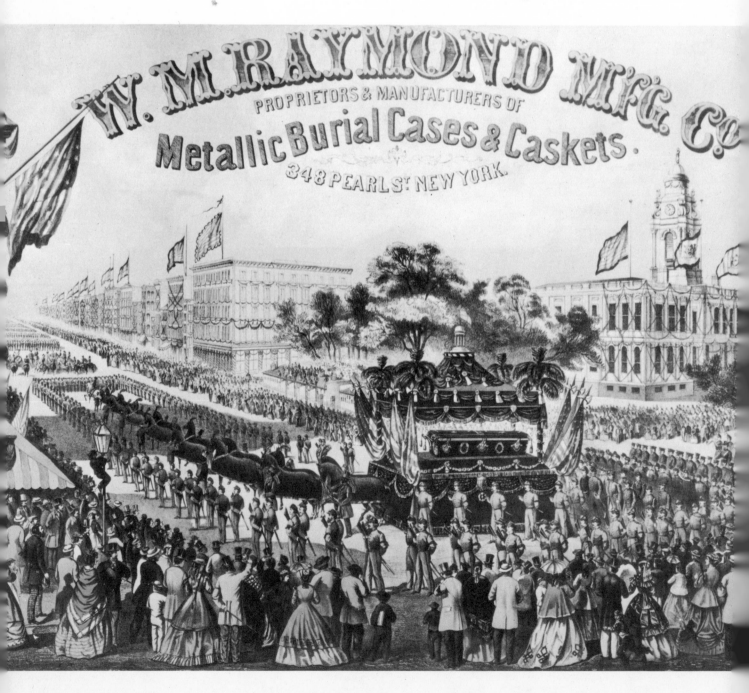

sive America's new interest in London, Paris, and Rome, they advertised California as "The Italy of America," Monterey Bay as "The Naples of the New World." Their arguments were competitive and persuasive. An overland journey was as pleasant as an ocean voyage—without the seasickness. American resorts were free of beggars, alien odors, avalanches (which purportedly dimmed one's enjoyment of the Alps), and, best of all, people spoke understandable English. Nature's grandeur, which had exacted its toll of exhausted pioneers a generation or two before, could now be savored without strain and within walking distance of expertly staffed hotels.

For the sportsmen there were camping trips de luxe. Roughing it, they drank champagne from tin cups and ate steaks prepared by a chef over the campfire. A critic said: "They could not ride (horses), and were too fat to walk." Neither exertion was necessary; they lounged in private railway cars that offered all the comforts of home and magnificent scenery as well.

New Englanders were offered five months at a Pacific resort for $750. They were promised not only a palatial drawing-room, but "select company." The traveler was assured that he would be "relieved of . . . proximity to . . . undesirable people."

While the elite could thus protect themselves from hoi polloi, ordinary folk enjoyed the crowded seaside resorts closer to home. The New Yorker's favorite was Coney Island, which offered a five-mile beach and a blessed bit of relief from the summer's heat. Bathing dress reflected the stifling modesty of the age: women wore black cotton stockings, navy blue or black suits with white trim, short puffed sleeves, ample skirts that ballooned in the water, and ruffled caps. Their escorts wore equally funereal colors, although stripes were permitted; their sleeves came to the elbow and their trunks to the knees. The all-over tan was far in the future.

For those surfeited with bathing, there were saloons, gambling houses, and other oases of refreshment along the strand. Before the subway cut the length of the trip to minutes, there was also a large hotel at which the affluent could spend the week end at ease, dining in splendor while watching the waves. For plebeian appetites, the ubiquitous hot dog was invented.

Coney Island's potential was not realized, however, until a master showman, George C. Tilyou, undertook to provide popular entertainment to go with the sea breezes. Tilyou started extracting money from the public by selling sea-water samples and sand to Midwesterners viewing the ocean for the first time. The Chicago World's Fair of 1893 spurred him to grander visions. He ordered a Ferris wheel for Coney, plus an aerial slide and a bicycle railway. Such was the beginning of Steeplechase Park.

Millions of people—generations of them—found the Coney Island attractions a never-ending delight. Competitors opened at locations nearby, but there was room for all. The more entertainment there was, the more customers came.

The American passion for self-improvement was not neglected at Coney. Stuffed whales, a flea circus, igloos, submarines, airplanes, and camels—all were there to be inspected and marveled at, for a fee.

On an even grander scale was the World's Fair. Here the might and money of the city was poured into a metropolitan version of the unfailingly popular county fair. New York, not surprisingly, started the fashion. Its Crystal Palace, a copy of the London original, opened in 1853. Cincinnati had a fair in the 1870's. Philadelphia, Chicago, Louisville, and more, sought to display the prowess and imagination and accomplishments of the self-confident Nineteenth Century.

Some never got off the ground. Some went bust. But all were fun. Philadelphia's celebrated the nation's hundredth birthday. Maestro Theodore Thomas, with an orchestra of two hundred and a chorus of a thousand voices, provided the music, although, to tell the truth, brass bands were more to the American taste.

President Grant, with the Emperor of Brazil beside him, started the huge Corliss steam engine whose forty miles of belt line powered all the machinery on exhibit. What astonished Emperor Dom Pedro most, however, and was, in fact, the hit of the exposition, was Alexander Graham Bell's telephone. Holding it to his ear, the Emperor gasped: "My God! It talks." At first, the telephone was viewed as little more than a wonderful toy. But, together with the fountain pen and the typewriter, it would one day become an essential tool of American business.

The most famous fair of the century was Chicago's. An American journalist said sententiously that it revealed to millions of his fellow citizens, "whose lives were necessarily colorless and narrow, the splendid possibilities of art and the compelling power of the beautiful." An English visitor rhapsodized that the Great White City of the exposition was "the greatest and most poetical dream that we have ever seen."

Twenty-seven million visitors came to admire the acres of landscaped parks, the long lagoons, and the white colonnades gleaming beside the blue waters of Lake Michigan. A marvelous fountain played at the entrance in the Court of Honor. The Ferris wheel lofted spectators into the sky for a bird's-eye view of the entire fair. The Midway, where George Tilyou paid close attention, offered Little Egypt's scandalous belly dance. And when the fair finally closed, there rose upon the Midway acres the University of Chicago. Its students sang:

The city white hath fled the earth,
But where the azure waters lie
A nobler city hath its birth,
A city gray that ne'er shall die.

Each fair struggled to out-do its predecessors. St. Louis, celebrating the centennial of the Louisiana Purchase, opened its Universal Exhibition in

City brownstones were all very similar.
Keeping them warm continued
to be a problem, even after the arrival of central heating.
Thick carpets and heavy draperies helped.

204

1904. Some twenty million people attended and were properly impressed, but perhaps the most memorable survivor of all the wonders on display was the ice-cream cone.

Although the fairs attracted visitors of all social and economic levels, it was noted that the Americans of this period were generally well dressed. Not richly, perhaps, but in a style whose uniformity bespoke the equality they felt. It was impossible to tell from clothes alone what a person's vocation might be, or whether he worked at all.

Much of America's clothing began to be store-bought soon after the middle of the Nineteenth Century. Stewart's, a spacious block-long New York store, was a favorite place to shop. By 1856 it added a fur department with "a large and well selected stock of . . . Cardinals, Victorines, Muffs, Cuffs, etc." Ready-made clothing was not new in America, but new inventions speeded up the change from homemade or tailor-made to ready-made. The hundred-thousand sewing machines that were manufactured annually transformed the clothing industry. A shirt that formerly took more than thirteen hours to make by hand could be made by machinery in an hour. A coat was made in three hours instead of seventeen.

The Civil War gave a tremendous lift to ready-made clothing when the Federal Government demanded, quickly, huge quantities of uniforms. Soldiers returning from the war found that stores were supplied with a variety of well-made civilian clothes to which they easily adjusted after wearing ready-made uniforms. The once spurned "hand-me-down" clothing (handed down from a clothing store rack) was now improved in tailoring and materials, and was accepted by people at all income levels. As women went to work in factories and offices they had little time to make clothes for themselves, and they, too, became mass purchasers of ready-mades.

An influx of immigrant tailors and seamstresses from eastern Europe helped bring about the new era in clothing for women. Conditions in the textile industry were harsh and unpleasant, but the labor of these industrious people produced an array of clothing at modest prices that enabled the average American woman to dress more stylishly on her budget than any other in the world.

Most women aspired to be fashionable and depended on *Godey's Lady's Book* for guidance. For half a century after it first appeared in 1830 it was the chief arbiter of fashions and etiquette. Paris fashions were still the model for American women, although they were adapted to New World tastes. Women's trousers for street wear, seen in Paris as early as 1810, were rejected by Americans for more than a century.

Ladies suffered tortures to be in style. They squeezed themselves into wasp waists, even though such pressure was said to be the cause of that "very fashionable disease—the liver complaint. Hence arise faintings in public assemblies." A bitter critic of corsets tried to shame women into giving them up. "Who does not know that compression of any part produces *Inflammation?* Who does not know that . . . tight-lacing around the waist . . . *inflames all the organs of the abdomen,* which thereby EXCITES AMATORY

*Lighting was revolutionized when
smoky lamps were replaced by gaslights. The central chandelier
was turned on and lit with the help of a long wand.*

Occasionally, disaster struck.
The fortunes of P.T. Barnum temporarily
were lost in a blaze that
destroyed his museum; the Panic of 1857 hit Wall Streeters
and shook the national economy.

Brightly shining engines of the volunteer fire companies were hauled through streets on the run when the alarm sounded.

DESIRES?" A virtuous woman, he went on, *"should blush for very shame to be laced tight, just as she should blush to be caught indulging impure desires."* Women may have blushed as they read the anti-corset crusader; they blushed often and with less reason. Nevertheless, they continued to pull in their waists as they stretched out on the floor, face downward, while another member of the household put one foot on their backs and tightened the laces of their stays.

In the 1840's and 1850's, a strong feminist movement in the United States prompted Amelia Bloomer to design the extraordinary garment that still bears her name. To ardent feminists, the "bloomer" was a symbol of woman's emancipation. It enabled her to reach a "position side by side with men . . . and give a more correct idea of the natural proportions of the human form." Although the defiant ones who launched the fashion were ridiculed by much of the country, bloomers persisted. Ultimately, they became standard wear for ladies engaging in gymnastics and athletic contests.

Another popular item of women's wear, although this made its appearance toward the end of the century, was the shirtwaist. Millions of them were sold in nearly every kind of fabric and often elaborately trimmed with lace insertions and embroidered medallions.

211

*Great mechanical
inventions and engineering feats
made the city easily
distinguishable from the town grown large.
Wondrous amusement parks were
erected and the newly-opened Brooklyn
Bridge was proclaimed
the eighth wonder of the world.*

The "Rainy Daisey," a ladies' walking skirt whose hem hovered two or three inches above the ground, was considered appropriate for street wear when it rained. The hem rose as bicycles became more popular and, although it was not high enough to reveal the cotton stocking above the high-button shoe, dire warnings were issued by the strait-laced about the fate in store for immodest women.

As for women's hats, one caustic reporter wrote that they "resembled nothing so much as the bird section of a museum of natural history, made up of thrushes, orioles, red-wing blackbirds, the gray mourning dove, the purplish-black grackle, the man-loving wren, and the common pigeon."

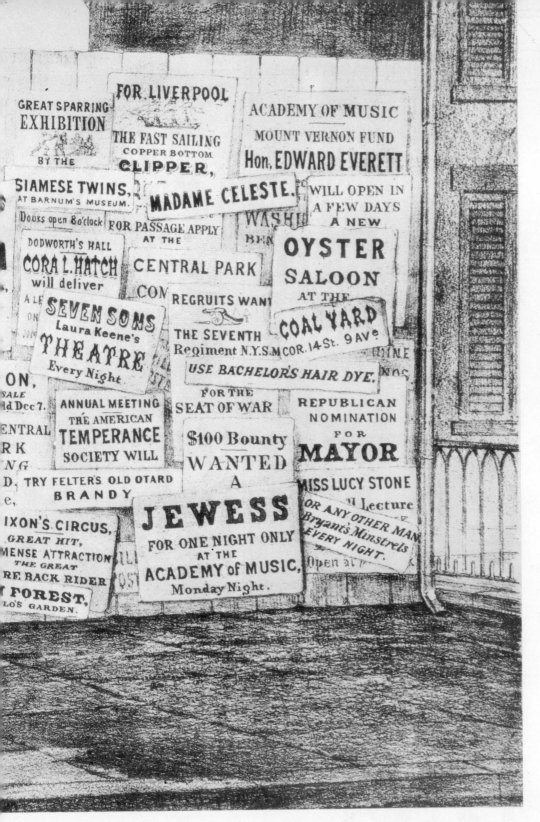

Posters announce a wide range of city activities. (Read vertically, they make weighty Nineteenth Century jokes.)

Actually, the choicest decoration for millinery was the plume of the egret.

Godey's Lady's Book urged women to keep in good physical condition as the first requisite of attractiveness. Beauty treatments were frowned on. The parasol was protection enough for a lovely complexion.

Drugstore nostrums would not brighten dull eyes or confer a clear skin, *Godey's* warned. "Splash the neck, chest, back, and face with cold water," it cried heartily. Women did, but they also continued to buy Dr. Campbell's Arsenic Complexion Wafers. Lackluster hair was to be "brushed well with oil well rubbed into the scalp." Women did this, too. Floor-length tresses were the ideal women everywhere sought to attain. And to hold her crowning

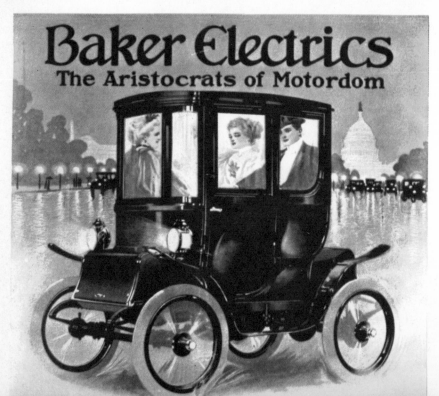

New vistas were opening for the fifth generation since Washington's inauguration. There were new enchantments and new complexities. The funnies became folk art. The electric car died. The airplane—and air war—bespoke the future.

glory in place, she employed hair nets, hairpins, back combs, side combs, and rat combs.

The use of "paint," although discouraged by *Godey's,* was discussed at length by other publications, for women found it a lively topic. Opponents asked: "Do those who redden their cheeks with *rouge,* darken their eyes, and cover their complexion with chalk, verily believe that they will call back the semblance of youth promised them by cosmetic concoctions?"

Apparently, they believed it implicitly. For even the farmer's wife was ordering rouge and French perfume from the mail-order catalogue. The opposition conceded that, "No one who has any idea of modern social life can deny that the use of all the adventitious aids to the toilet which have been condemned since the days of Jezebel—paint, powder, enamel, hair-dye, and every other kind of 'beautifier'—is enormously on the increase in society. They seem to have attractions for all ages," including "tender little rosebuds." Discreet and artistic make-up was not too severely condemned, although if applied crudely it would stamp "the most honest woman . . . as 'fast.'"

Before World War I, make-up had become acceptable to most women. Although some were still hesitant, they gradually yielded to "artifice." Young girls, however, were allowed only an occasional powdering of cornstarch. Rouge for them was unthinkable. Before 1914 a young girl with artificially red cheeks might be followed by children jeering: "Her mother lets her pai-ent, her mother lets her pai-ent."

If there was still some hesitation about improving nature above the neck, no such scruples halted alterations just below. A fashionable woman wanted a large bust to emphasize her wasp waist. But while the natural form could be compressed by corsets, how to enlarge it? One could not be sure, but one could try: "IF NATURE HAS NOT FAVORED YOU with that greatest charm, a symmetrically rounded bosom full and perfect, send for the Princess Bust Developer."

Men, as well as women, were criticized for paying excessive attention to their appearance. "There has been of late years," wrote a critic in the mauve decade of the 1890's, "much talk about the 'mannish' woman, but it is well to remember that she is closely rivaled by the womanish or 'ladylike' man. . . . Paint, powder, perfumes, dyes, irons for waving and curling their exquisite mustaches . . . scented sachets to fasten inside their coats . . . all these and many other items . . . form part of the indispensable 'get-up' of our modern society man."

A more general male fashion which became popular about the middle of the century was the beard. Styles were many, from the trim little Vandyke to the enormous spade beard that fell to the chest. General Ambrose Burnside was the originator of sideburns. Handlebar mustaches that drooped abruptly at the corners of the mouth were known as "Over Niagara."

As the century neared its close, beards vanished and the mustache carried on alone. The ends were curled or twirled to a waxed point.

Charles Dana Gibson changed the whole situation overnight. All male America was in love with the Gibson girl, and when the artist drew her escort as clean-shaven, mustaches—and mustache-cups—were doomed.

Male fashions accentuated the shoulders. Coats were heavily padded. The gallant wore fancy silk or wash vests; the clerk at his desk donned a black alpaca coat. Formal daytime wear called for a cutaway coat, gray striped trousers, and a stovepipe hat. The derby was standard for ordinary wear, except in the summer, when a stiff, straw boater with a striped band was considered spiffy.

The Federal Government
deserted New York in 1790 and dashed
the city's hopes of
being the national capital. But its air of
excitement made it a
show place, anyway. Broadway
beguiled the innocent and unwary; the
Hippodrome housed spectacles.

Men's "stretchy seam drawers"—ankle-length—underlay all this high fashion. Also the tan undershirt, with sleeves to the wrist. Or one might favor the one-piece union suit. Heavy cotton or wool was customary in winter, usually red to cure rheumatic pains.

Dress shirts had stiff, white, detachable collars. They were worn high and, after a few launderings, had rasping edges that sandpapered a gentleman's neck. For the thrifty there were celluloid collars that did not wilt and could be cleaned with a swipe of a wet sponge. Detachable collars and cuffs enabled the fastidious to freshen a shirt without actually changing it.

On Sunday, the whole family dressed up. Mother wore her best black silk dress and plumed hat, father his black coat, striped pants, and gray gloves, and he carried a gold-headed cane. Small boys wore knee-pants, a sailor's middy blouse, and a round hat. Little girls favored white dresses with pink sashes. All prim and proper.

Most cities at the turn of the century were strict about their Blue Laws. Sunday was meant for religion, but slowly the day began more and more to mean recreation, indoors and out. Sunday morning still was reserved for church and Sunday school. Then home to the Sunday paper. Its bright Colored Supplement livened the day. Buster Brown, Happy Hooligan, Foxy Grandpa, and the Katzenjammer Kids were among the favorite "funnies." (Rights to the Yellow Kid, an early comic strip, caused a bitter conflict between Hearst and Pulitzer, out of which came the phrase "yellow journalism.")

St. Nicholas Magazine was the approved reading for children. It had a strong moral flavor and was designed to furnish home amusement with games, stories, and articles about exploration and science. Its pictures were as important as its text. While it enjoyed great popularity for many years, it had serious competition. Dime novels had avid readers, both young and old. Boys risked being sent to bed without supper if caught reading about Nick Carter and Deadwood Dick.

Outdoor activities centered on the city parks. There the rich rode horseback along soft bridle paths or drove their carriages along shady roads. Ordinary folk gave their children a chance to ride brightly painted mechanical horses on the carousel and bought them peanuts to feed to the elephant in the zoo. Popcorn and balloons made the holiday complete.

Croquet enjoyed great popularity. Golf was taking hold here and there. Professional baseball was on the verge of becoming the national pastime. But the supreme sport of the Nineties was bicycling. Everyone who could manage to buy, borrow, or rent a bike was out on the road at every opportunity. Roller-skating rinks and dance halls were taken over by people learning to ride. The sports pages of the newspapers reported bicycle races to the fullest. A race from Chicago to Pullman, Illinois, drew a thousand entries, many in the professional rider's close-fitting black tights. Society columns reported socialite outings to the country club. Bicycle clubs abounded. Parking bikes in the city was an acute problem.

The bicycle enabled you to travel when and where you wished. The pneumatic tires provided a smooth, silent ride that was infinitely pleasing, and when you turned on the speed—"scorching"—you could do ten miles an

Genteel Philadelphia lost its position as the nation's premier city, but was satisfied with its mercantile success, its cultural attainments, and a secure place in history.

*Dapper New Yorkers
model the Anthony Adverse fashions
of the 1830's, available
at an early Brooks Brothers'
store. Remington made sewing
machines as well as guns.*

hour with ease. Pedestrians and horses drew back before an oncoming caravan of bicycle-club riders and dogs barked in a frenzy and chased the silvery, spinning wheels.

For those whose funds would not carry them far, there were excursion boats on the lakes and rivers. Sunday crowds went to the trolley parks. They clambered aboard the horse-drawn, open-air trolleys and rode to the end of the line where an amusement park with picnic grove, beer garden, ball field, and grandstand awaited.

For the city-bound, there was the "Y." Here the lonesome newcomer, particularly, could feel assured of a moral atmosphere where he could meet others feeling the pangs that came from leaving familiar surroundings to live in a community of strangers. Loneliness was a common affliction in those days. At the Chicago World's Fair, the one picture that consistently drew a crowd was Thomas Hovenden's "Breaking the Home Ties" which showed a farm boy leaving for the city. The pensive viewers knew the feeling.

The institution of the summer vacation was becoming established. People's means and opportunities differed, but there were resorts and tourist attractions for every pocketbook and every taste.

Maple Terrace House, of Milton, New York, advertised: "Young people wanted; gay crowd, dancing, boating, bathing, fishing, piano, hammocks, shade, excellent table; leave old folks to hum."

For more sedate groups, there were family lodgings, inns, farms, and beach cottages that promised the pleasures of the outdoors. New Yorkers liked going to New England by steamer through Long Island Sound. The sporting set went to Saratoga for the races. Flat track, that is. Harness races were at Goshen. The wealthy gathered at Saratoga's Grand Union Hotel or the United States, and sat and rocked on the "millionaires' piazzas," smoking and talking and watching the world go by. Others visited the famous springs to drink the curative waters. Others were there frankly to gamble. "Diamond Jim" Brady, who sported a new set of jewels every day of the month, and "Bet-a-Million" Gates, the most spectacular plunger at Canfield's, caused a stir whenever they appeared.

The real money went to Newport or to Bar Harbor. No advertising here. Newport's Bailey Beach excluded all but the *crème de la crème*. Lawn tennis and golf were the pastimes of the industrialists and merchant princes who came to pass the summer in their mansions.

Bar Harbor was for the yachting set. Ever since America had defeated Britain for the America Cup in 1851, yacht racing had had international overtones, and millionaires combined in syndicates to build up and race ever-faster boats that would maintain American supremacy. The yacht, like the private railroad car, was a hallmark of wealth. When J. P. Morgan was asked how much it cost to maintain a yacht, he answered imperiously: "If you have to ask, you can't afford it." With even greater hauteur, the old titan announced that, "You can do business with anyone, but you can only sail a boat with a gentleman."

One needed no chit from Mr. Morgan to visit the seat of American

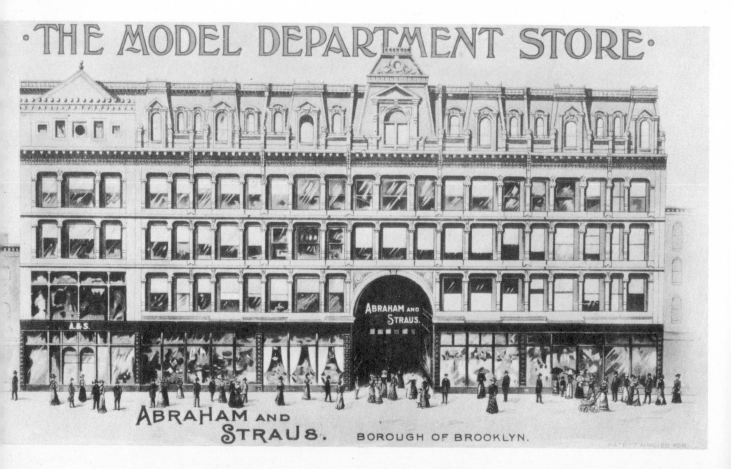

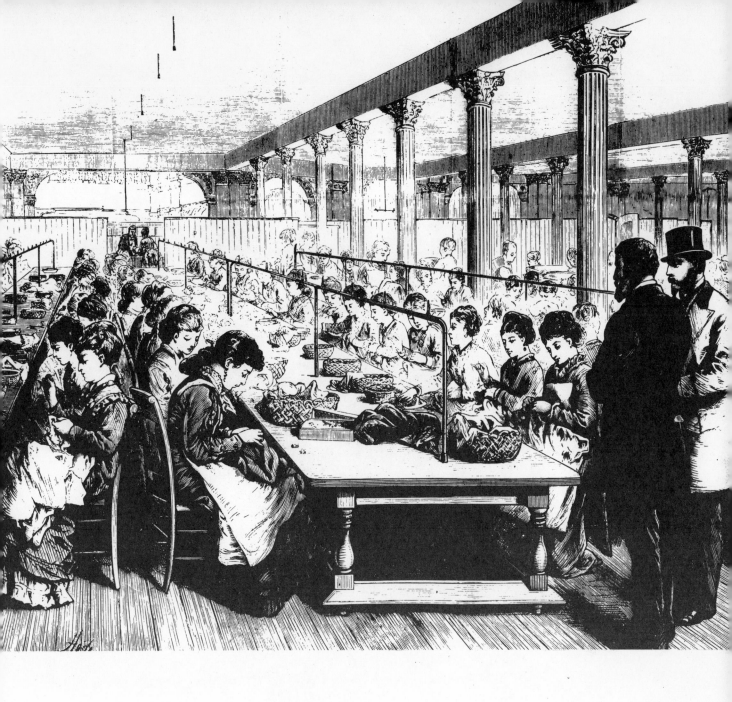

That great merchandising emporium,
the department store, was born just before the Civil
War. A. T. Stewart's was among the first
and most famous. Its sewing room employed an army of
girls to finish and alter ladies'
clothing. Another innovation, the mail-order
house, competed with the country store by offering
tempting wares in gaudy catalogues.

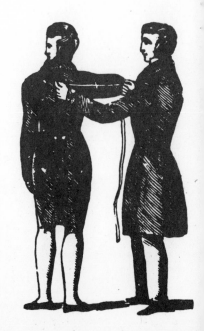

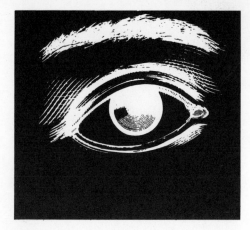

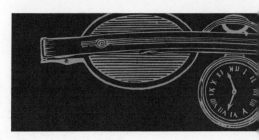

democracy, however, and an endless stream of people visited Washington, D.C., in all seasons to see the buildings and monuments that personified the freedom they enjoyed.

Every section of the country had its spectacle and the trains bulged with easterners going west and westerners coming east to see Pike's Peak, Yellowstone Park and Old Faithful geyser, Arizona's Grand Canyon, Atlantic City's boardwalk, New York's Statue of Liberty, Chinatown, ocean liners in port, Broadway theaters, and subways.

Honeymooners went to Niagara Falls, as did visitors from all over the world. Everyone was impressed, save, perhaps, Oscar Wilde, who was rarely overwhelmed. "Isn't it wonderful?" he was asked by an enthusiastic member of his party. "Hmm," he granted. "But think how much more wonderful if it fell up instead of down."

Of course, some folks lived high all the year around. Their mansions could be seen, from a distance, on the Long Island shore, at Tuxedo Park, or on Fifth Avenue. At Lenox, Massachusetts, Anson P. Stokes built "Shadowbrook," a turreted, granite castle with one hundred rooms that permitted a truly lavish scale of hospitality. "Arriving this evening with crowd of ninety-six men," wired a young Stokes from Yale. "Many guests already here," mother wired back. "Have only room for fifty."

As the new century got under way, New York society was a mixture of Ward McAllister's selected "Four Hundred" and many whose new fortunes from oil, railroads, and "trade" gave them hopes of crashing the gates. Some of the "steel barons, coal lords, dukes of wheat and beef" had managed to get in even before the turn of the century.

The society columns of the newspapers told in glittering detail of the

226

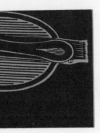

goings on in the Gilded Age. They reported a dazzling ball given in 1897 by the Bradley Martins at the Waldorf-Astoria. The hotel's interior had been turned into a copy of Versailles, with rare tapestries and flowers. "I do not think that there has ever been a greater display of jewels," said a relative of the hosts. But the panic of Ninety-three was still fresh in the public mind. Newspapers turned on the Martins for a wanton and tasteless display. The Martins left for Europe.

The rich still liked to spend money. In 1905, Mrs. Astor gave a ball at her home for four-hundred-and-fifty guests. And other parties featured breath-takingly sumptuous decor: an artificial waterfall in a private dining room to delight dinner guests; a mass of three thousand roses to decorate a table; nightingales to furnish background music; acts from a Broadway show; a costume ball with the Metropolitan Opera orchestra to furnish music.

In Chicago, Mrs. Potter Palmer wanted the noted composer, Richard Strauss, to play a few numbers for her dinner guests and used all her influence, plus $5,000, to get him. Some elaborate parties were rumored to cost $100,000. Eventually, the moneyed aristocracy of America gained entrée to the blooded aristocracy of Europe, and international marriages conferred desirable titles on the daughters of tycoons. The marriage in 1874 of Miss Jennie Jerome to Lord Randolph Churchill, the parents of Sir Winston, set the style.

The top layers of wealth could not obscure the wretched conditions that existed below and, often, improvements came only after epidemic or fire had struck. Starting afresh after devastation, cities enforced better sanitation and rewrote their antiquated building codes.

Fire destroyed most American cities at one time or another. The wood out of which most of them were built in the earlier years was tinder to the torch. New York was largely burnt down during the Revolution, rebuilt and leveled again in 1835. A generation later one of the greatest fires in American history wiped out much of Chicago. The alarm sounded on Sunday night, October 8, 1871. Legend blames the fire on Mrs. O'Leary's cow, which kicked over a lantern.

In a short time the flames were moving "like ocean surf on a sand beach," wrote a Chicago journalist. Families hurried through the choked streets dragging trunks or with piles of clothing on their shoulders. Many died screaming on burning roof tops. Rows of houses fell before the flames like "ripe wheat before the reaper." To make fire breaks, block after block was dynamited. Pumps failed and firemen found their hoses empty. The flames roared for two days and nights through three-and-a-half square miles, destroying over 17,000 buildings; damage to property was placed at some $200,000,000. Two hundred people were killed. One of every four residents

in the city of 300,000 was left homeless. Huddled in Lincoln Park with smoke-blackened faces, they were thankful to be alive.

Within a few years Chicago leaped from its ashes more speedily than it had once risen from the prairie. Brick residences and imposing stone structures replaced wood. Carl Sandburg's "City of the Big Shoulders" was reborn.

On the Pacific Coast, San Francisco, high on its hills, was a reality beyond the wildest dream. It was built with the gold from California's mines, the harvests of its golden fields, and the wealth of the railroads that brought a constant stream of people and freight to its doors. Stately ships home from China anchored in its magnificent bay and gave the city such flavor as no other in America possessed. But San Francisco, too, was prone to fire. A newspaperman visiting San Francisco in the 1860's marveled that although it had "burned to the ground six times," it had recovered quickly to enjoy even greater prosperity.

Electricity lights New York's
Grand Street at nine o'clock on a rainy evening.
On week ends, the horsecar offered
outings to end-of-the-line
parks and playgrounds. Hatters now sold
bowlers. Stovepipes were passé.

229

The blow that came in 1906 was more savage than any before. On April 18, in early morning, an earthquake rocked the city. Tenement houses fell to the ground. Walls were skinned off great steel buildings. Cable-car tracks were bent and flung about. Fire fed by broken gas mains spread quickly. With water mains broken, firemen used dynamite. Stricken people fled to the parks to escape falling walls; they screamed and moaned with each successive shock. The Palace Hotel, built in 1875 at a cost of $5,000,000, was completely destroyed. Crazed men and women fought each other for the safety of an open square. For four days the holocaust raged over five square miles, killing five hundred people, consuming over 28,000 buildings, destroying property worth a billion dollars.

After a period of shock, the city gathered its resources and the miracle of rebirth occurred once more. Again there arose the enchanting city by the Golden Gate, more resplendent than before.

Modernity came to the cities. No longer were they simply the town grown large. Great mechanical inventions were applied to the particular requirements of city living, great engineering feats solved—and sometimes complicated—the problems that the city's structure imposed. In the late 1870's, over violent opposition, New York undertook to span the East River with a bridge to Brooklyn. Many of Manhattan's workers hitherto had commuted across the river by ferry, the sole link between the boroughs. A bridge would give swift and convenient access to the city, particularly in bad weather, when fog and ice delayed the ferries.

The opposition complained of the expense and viewed the project as another opportunity for political boondoggling by Tammany Hall. It was swept aside.

The bridge took seven years to build. (The opposition was at least half right.) John Roebling, the chief engineer, died before it was completed and his son, Washington, who carried on, himself became ill and directed the work from the window of his room overlooking the river.

On May 24, 1883, the bridge was opened with one of the largest celebra-

Godey's Lady's Book *was the foremost arbiter in matters of fashion for women and young children.*

tions in any city's history. Flags waved, cannon boomed, crowds cheered. Roebling, still confined to his chair, received President Chester A. Arthur and a clutch of governors, mayors, and distinguished visitors come to congratulate him on "this eighth wonder of the world."

Cities now were enveloped in sound. Traffic was beyond control. And in progressive cities, like New York and Chicago, the elevated railroad contributed to the din. The "el" speeded transportation, but it darkened the streets and sometimes dropped hot cinders that started fires in the wagons passing underneath.

Increasing traffic forced New York to think of going underground to find routes for rapid transit. Europe had already done so, and so had Boston. After four years of labor, the subway in New York was opened to the public on October 27, 1904. The next morning, *The New York Times* reported that "for the first time in his life Father Knickerbocker went underground yesterday . . . to the number of 150,000 amid the tooting of whistles and the firing of salutes. . . ." Mayor McClellan, with a silver controller, started the first train "at 2:35.30 o'clock yesterday afternoon." It was carnival night in town, with celebrations in Times Square and at City Hall Park. The *Times* exulted that in less than half an hour passengers would be carried a dozen miles from City Hall. Looking to the future of the metropolitan area, it prophesied that the transit system would make possible a population of ten millions.

Nothing overhauled the nation's habits and patterns, however, so much as the automobile. Its arrival in the final years of the century was lightly regarded, but spluttering, cantankerous, and imperfect as it was, it had a potential that an industrial nation could recognize and develop. The earliest

*Every red-blooded American male was
in love with the Gibson girl. She personified style, grace,
and elegance Americans were delighted to
know they possessed. Her clean-shaven escort single-
handedly doomed U.S. beards and mustaches.*

cars ran on the century's most familiar motive power—steam. But the growing oil industry would soon be geared to fuel the internal combustion engine. The steel, rubber, glass, and electrical-products industries would soon grow great at least in part through the manufacture of automobile elements. And highway construction would resurface the nation, providing routes to every destination that whim, commerce, or aspiration might choose.

None of this happened immediately. But nothing proved the dynamism of what grandfather was pleased to call "automobility" more than the fact that it happened at all.

The beginnings were unpromising. Early automobiles were expensive. Many people were utterly convinced that they were dangerous. The backlash of a balky engine broke many a cranking arm. Tires blew. Brakes failed. Horrific speeds could lead only to disaster. Organized opposition threw many obstacles in the way. Influential citizens blocked legislation to provide new roads lest the native charm of their communities be spoiled. Road signs were lacking. Maps were unavailable.

Yet the exhilaration of riding a "horseless" made converts of everyone who tried it. Cars sat high on the road, making the driver lord of creation. Dust swirled in his face, but, undaunted, he outfitted himself with duster, goggles, gauntlets, and cap, and swathed his lady in flowing veils.

Somehow, traveling at speed outweighed the absence of service stations and competent mechanics, the wretchedness of quagmire roads, and the ridicule of the uninitiated. "Get a horse," they jeered. But they were riding their buggies and carriages to oblivion. For despite the exasperating breakdowns, the automobile was the vehicle of the free man, the fitting symbol of the free, forward-looking, fast-moving society.

Women's approval of the new machine was perhaps the deciding factor. Within a few years, they, too, were driving, although usually with a man aboard to take care of cranking and repairs. The one car a woman could take out by herself was the electric brougham: its hard-rubber tires never

Washington reminded Americans of the

freedom they enjoyed. A small city family observed

Thanksgiving quietly. Mr. Edison and Mr. Smith

transformed the secretary's life.

You Can Bathe in California

At any time of year and at almost any point on the coast. But the strong probability is that you won't. There are other things to do that are better worth doing—and, besides, there are better places to bathe than in the cool waters of the Pacific.

All along the coast—at San Diego, Coronado, Santa Barbara, Monterey and a dozen other places that might be named, luxurious bath houses have been built, where the water, fresh from the sea, is heated and tempered to your liking. The way to get to California is via

The Golden State Limited

which runs over the

Rock Island System,
Chicago and Kansas City to Santa Rosa.

El Paso-Northeastern System,
Santa Rosa to El Paso.

Southern Pacific,
El Paso to Los Angeles and San Francisco.

Leaves Chicago daily on and after December 20. Arrives Los Angeles sixty-eight hours later. Finest equipment on wheels—standard and compartment sleepers, dining, buffet-smoking-library and observation cars. Fully described in our California literature, ready December 1, and sent for 6 cents in stamps.

JOHN SEBASTIAN,
Passenger Traffic Manager,
CHICAGO, ILL.

G.A.R

A winter freeze has

brought skaters to Central Park since pre-Civil War

days. Modestly attired vacationers

of a later era bathed in Atlantic breakers or

basked in California's year-around sun.

blew out, it couldn't go fast or far, it was genteel and safe. Its huge batteries needed continual recharging, however, and, like the steamers, it would prove to be short-lived.

A handsome and memorable variety of cars was produced in America in the first decade of the Twentieth Century, but it was the Ford that assured the automobile's place in the nation's life. The Model T "Tin Lizzie" was an extraordinary car, yet even more remarkable was the assembly-line technique of production that enabled Mr. Ford to bring his car within reach of everyone. While the price of other cars still ranged in the thousands, Ford was charging less than $400—and making one of America's great fortunes, to boot.

The triumph of the automobile was assured. Steadily, the faithful horse lost status, although horsepower remained the gauge of the car's output. Declining with him was a vast army of specialists that for generations had derived a livelihood from attendance to his needs: coachmen, postilions, grooms, blacksmiths, wheelwrights, harness and saddle makers, coach builders, feed merchants, and the anonymous artisans who made spurs, hitching posts, watering troughs, buggy whips, horse collars, bits, surcingles, feedbags, and curry combs. Some, like the coach builders, might find their talents adaptable

*Indoor sports included roller skating
to music of a balcony orchestra, and big-league bowling at old Madison
Square Garden. The bicycle craze of the 1890's
saw rinks and dance halls converted for riding lessons.*

to the construction or servicing of the automobile, but the others would be a vanishing breed.

For a while the horse survived on the farm, yet even there his chores increasingly were performed by the motorized tractor, by tireless, self-powered machinery. As a rural poet said:

> *Things are changing over our way*
> *Better than they were by far,*
> *No more longing; no more sighing;*
> *Father's gone and bought a car.*
>
> *But we've sold our mules and horses,*
> *All those beasts have had their day,*
> *Father merely smokes and mentions,*
> *"Take the Ford and rake the hay."*

Adjustment of the national psyche to the automobile made acceptance of the airplane easy. Although the possibility of the earth-bound becoming airborne was highly exciting, it was a plus, an extra, an almost superfluous miracle that a people capable of hurtling itself at sixty miles an hour or more could take with equanimity.

The wish to fly was of long standing. Between 1800 and 1859 there had been three thousand balloon ascensions attesting to the impulse. Few were

Homes were jammed with creature comforts. Soda fountains served a new drink.

the fairgrounds that did not offer a balloon ride to the daring. In 1859, one John Wise was entrusted with the first U.S. mail to travel by balloon. During the Civil War the Union army sent up balloons for reconnaissance of enemy positions. But all attempts to fly in powered, heavier-than-air machines failed until December, 1903.

The Wright brothers, Orville and Wilbur, had always been preoccupied with the problem of flight. As youngsters they were expert kite flyers. As young men they read everything available on the as yet unsolved problem. They talked with men who had pondered the requirements of flight. And they built models to see what they could learn of the principles of aerodynamics. In 1900 they intensified their efforts, setting up on the dunes of Kitty Hawk, North Carolina, and conducting experimental glider flights at nearby Kill Devil Hill. In 1902, they made nearly a thousand glides, "coasting downhill on the air," to practice balancing a flying machine, which they considered to be a vital element of the problem. In 1903, they made their first flight in a

240

powered machine. It was a skeleton biplane that stayed aloft for twelve seconds. For the first time in man's history a machine had risen into the air, flown a level course without reducing speed, and made a safe landing. Their fourth flight lasted nearly a minute and covered eight-hundred-and-fifty-two feet against a twenty-mile-an-hour wind.

There was still much to learn, but the idea was feasible. In a decade the airplane evolved sufficiently to be used as a dramatic weapon in World War I. In the years to come it would be a commonplace serving to cut still further the time and distance between cities.

The great war of 1914 burst upon the world one-hundred-and-thirty-five years after George Washington was inaugurated as the first President of the United States. Each of those years, taken by itself, was not greatly different from the one that preceded it or the one that followed. Even decades had similarities that survived from one to the other. But in human

Suddenly, everyone was mad
for bicycles. Week ends, the highways were thronged with
cycling clubs en route to the country
for an outing. In town, the
traffic was dreadful and parking a problem.

THE YELLOW BOOK

AUGUST

5 CENTS

Sydney Adamson

HOWARD,
AINSLEE & C?.

PUBLISHERS
NEW YORK

*The moving stairway, electric streetcar,
and elevated train were metropolitan marvels that colored the
countryman's dream of glamorous city living.*

terms, four generations had elapsed and the fifth was the child of a new
century. Between its outlook and that of its predecessors the chasm was
vast. It had continuity, of course, but its memory would not reach very far
back. Among its elders were some who had heard Lincoln speak. There
were grandfathers who could tell brave tales of finding gold in California.
But anything earlier than that would have to be the transmitted memories
of still others.

Like most generations just beginning it would look forward, not back.
It would believe its prospects good, although feeling its problems to be
great. If it did not always relish change, it would be accepting of it, for
change often brought a sophistication of implements and ideas that enabled
people of sense and good will to fend off the tigers that assail civilization.

Statistically, the changes over the years since Washington were enormous.
The infant republic's thirteen states had become forty-eight with the entrance
of Arizona into the Union in 1912. The four million newly independent
Americans of 1789 had become more than ninety million. The four per cent
that lived in the few cities of the late Eighteenth Century had swelled to
fifty in the urban centers of the Twentieth.

Technological differences were almost beyond comprehension. Machinery

had increased enormously the speed and volume of production. Each man had more kilowatts of power working for him than ever before in history. There was little in the economic complex of 1914 that an American who had welcomed the Nineteenth Century's dawn would find familiar.

Yet for each generation there had been and would be an accumulating inheritance. The past lived in the present and would lend its impulse to the construction of the future. It was an inheritance intangible, but pervasive, and it conferred on all who felt it a perspective, a consistency, a sense of identity. Applied to national deeds and purposes, the inheritance could be called patriotism. But it embodied more than this, even as the past was more than its heroes. For it was the rhythms and urgencies and significances of everyday living that gave fullness to the gift and made yesterday the friend of tomorrow.

The city man of 1914 could never know the pinching cold of a New England church on an Eighteenth Century Sunday. The countryman visualized a different New York than his forebears. The villager no longer trekked to Oregon; he lived there. Nonetheless, as each looked ahead, accoutred for the march with the airplanes, automobiles, and appliances symbolizing his time, he would carry within him a distillation of all that had gone before. He would feel the emotions of many regions, many people, and many years, and know himself to be an American.

The Pierce-Arrow

Sheridan

With the arrival of the automobile,
the world would never be the same again. Here was the noisy,
shining, irresistible symbol of the Twentieth
Century that would banish the horse.

PICTURE SOURCES   We wish to thank the following museums,
libraries, societies, individuals, and dealers through whose courtesy
the pictures on the pages listed below were reproduced.

BROOKLYN MUSEUM: top 73; top 155.

COLLECTION OF EDGAR WILLIAM
AND BERNICE CHRYSLER GARBISCH: top 124.

KENNEDY GALLERIES, INC., NEW YORK: top 16; bottom 23; bottom 60.

KING FEATURES SYNDICATE: top 216.

M. KNOEDLER & CO., INC., NEW YORK: top 60.
METROPOLITAN MUSEUM OF ART, NEW YORK:
bottom 38 (Rogers Fund, 1907); 57 (Gift of Mr. and Mrs. Carl Stoeckel, 1897);
bottom 74 (Gift of Miss A. S. Colgate, 1951); top 121 (Lazarus Fund, 1922);
132 (Bequest of Collis B. Huntington, 1925, and
Gift of John D. Crimmins, 1897); 147 (Lyman G. Bloomingdale, 1901);
top 157 (Gift of Christian A. Zabriskie, 1950); 172, 182,
top 184, 188, 202, top 208 (All from Edward W. C. Arnold Collection.
Photos Courtesy of Museum of the City of New York);
top 204 (Gift of Colonel Charles A. Fowler, 1921);
bottom 204 (Gift of Frederick A. Hatch, 1926);
213 (Alfred N. Punnett Fund, 1939).

MISSOURI HISTORICAL SOCIETY, ST. LOUIS: bottom right 40.

MUSEUM OF THE CITY OF NEW YORK
(Including Harry T. Peters Collection): top 13; bottom 16; 21-22;
bottom 24; top 30; 49; 52; top 58; 68-69; bottom 73; 75; bottom 84; 88;
middle and bottom 96; 114; top 125; 129; bottom 135; 148; 150; 153;
bottom 158; bottom 175; 181; bottom 208; top 210; 211;
bottom 212; top 213; top 223.

MUSEUM OF FINE ARTS, BOSTON (M. & M. Karolik Collection):
bottom 42-43; top 44; 102; 111; bottom 121; bottom 124; 174; top 191.

NATIONAL ACADEMY OF DESIGN, NEW YORK: 128.

NATIONAL GALLERY OF ART, WASHINGTON, D. C.
(From the Collection of American Primitive Paintings Given by
Edgar William and Bernice Chrysler Garbisch):
jacket and title page; bottom 17; bottom 28.

NEWARK MUSEUM: bottom 77; 163; bottom 165; top 168.

NEW YORK PUBLIC LIBRARY (Including Stokes and Eno Collections):
top 23; top 24; 27 (except bottom right); top 28; top 31; 32; bottom 33;
34 (except middle right); bottom 44; 54; bottom 67; middle 77;
top 83; 98; 99; bottom 100; top 104; 106; 112-113; top right 114;
bottom 118; 127; bottom 138; 150; 166; 167; 170; 173; 176; 184-185;
top 187; 190; bottom 191; bottom 196; 197; 214-215; 218; 219; bottom 236.

NEW YORK HISTORICAL SOCIETY
(Including Bella K. Landauer Collection): top 17; top right 35;
top 38; 50; 53; bottom 55; 56; bottom right 65; top 74;
top 78; top 82; 85; 86; 89; 91; 92-93; top 96; middle 107; top 108;
117; 130; 135; 139; 146; 149; 151; 160-161; 164; 171; 189;
209; right 216; 221; 222; 238; 239; 240.

OLD PRINT SHOP, NEW YORK: 94; 95; 103; 116; 123; 145;
top 158; top 201; middle 223.

PHILADELPHIA MUSEUM OF ART: bottom 157.

ABBY ALDRICH ROCKEFELLER FOLK ART COLLECTION,
WILLIAMSBURG, VA.: top 55.